"News is not like sausage. People love to see how it's put together. This book is the ultimate inside look at the pressures of daily decision-making at a small newspaper. It belongs on the desks of reporters and editors and is a must for news junkies."

— Arlin Albrecht, Publisher (retired), *Red Wing Republican Eagle*

"At a time when too many publishers and editors take pains to keep tough stories out of their newspapers, Pumarlo's commitment to reporting community news that makes some people in town uncomfortable pays crucial respect to journalism's mission."

— Gary Gilson, Executive Director, Minnesota News Council

"This book should be on the desk of every community newspaper editor. You'll be glad you have Jim Pumarlo's experienced guidance whenever you face a tough ethical decision. Should we publish this accident scene photo? Should we print the name of the local executive who committed suicide? You will feel much more confident making these decisions after reading this book.

"To help you as you review or develop your policies on covering sensitive issues, Jim has included a section with sample policy language. Why reinvent the wheel when an experienced editor can guide you in your task?"

— Linda Falkman, Executive Director, Minnesota Newspaper Association

Bad News and
Good Judgment

A Guide to Reporting on Sensitive Issues in a Small-Town Newspaper

Jim Pumarlo

Marion Street Press, Inc.
Oak Park, Illinois

Library of Congress Cataloging-in-Publication Data

pending

Cover photo by Colin Beltz, used with permission of
the *Red Wing Republican Eagle*

ISBN 0-9665176-1-X
Printed in U.S.A.
Printing 10 9 8 7 6 5 4 3 2

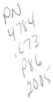

Marion Street Press, Inc.
PO Box 2249
Oak Park, IL 60303
866-443-7987
www.marionstreetpress.com

To my parents for their support, especially my dad who challenged me to always strive for an "A,"

To my high school adviser, Brent Norlem, who instilled in me the spirit of journalism,

To general managers Jim Edlund and Dave Ramnes, who provided me opportunities to grow,

To attorney Mark Anfinson, a confidant who offered guidance in press law and ethics,

To my publishers Arlin Albrecht and Phil Duff, who defined the best in community journalism in this nation,

To my wife Diane, for her unending encouragement.

Contents

Introduction
Connecting with readers

One of the endearing characteristics of hometown journalism is that loyal readers love to hate their editor. That's because grassroots editors have to make the call on stories that involve friends, neighbors and the person who sits across the table at Kiwanis — not to mention members of their families.

As I began writing this book, I spent an afternoon reviewing various letters and files accumulated throughout my 28 years in the newspaper business, the last 22 as editor of the *Red Wing Republican Eagle* in Minnesota. Two stood out:

From a reporter, who ranked among the best that I had the opportunity to oversee, upon acceptance of another job: "I learned about fighting hard for what's public, writing tough stories and never letting up when it comes to getting information and remaining on top of the news. I have never worked with anybody who pushes as hard as you do for the big and small information that some would keep from the public. A lot of reporters and editors talk the talk, but you walk the talk. I learned a lot watching you do that, even if it aggravated the hell out of me sometimes."

From an anonymous reader, clearly upset with newspaper coverage: "I don't know any of these three people personally whose lives you have taken upon yourself to ruin. But from the people I talk to, whether they know these people or not, they have the feeling of sympathy for their very public tongue-lashing from you. ... Maybe you should get a job with the 'Enquirer' or some 'rag' like that. That seems to be where your talent and your heart lies (reporting vicious gossip). Please step aside and let a real editor print the news."

Readers send favorable letters, too. But the stack of brickbats easily dwarfs the compliments. The imbalance of comments should surprise no one who has been in the business.

Often, the responses prompted us to examine our policies in the calm that comes after the daily crush of deadlines. Reader comments provided a platform to explain the hows and whys of news decisions.

Questions raised by readers became the foundation for my weekly column — an avenue to help readers better understand the dynamics of our decisions. Some columns staunchly defended our positions. Some reported adjustments in our policies. And others simply said, "We goofed."

Small-town editors routinely find themselves in no-win situations. No matter what they pursue in a news story, or write in an editorial, someone will be upset. Editors are expected to extol the virtues of their communities, so they incur the wrath of readers when they expose the warts and pimples — even when that exposure is good for the community.

The strongest and most defensible newspaper decisions are those grounded in well-developed policies. At the same time, the human element cannot be overlooked. Editors should not follow policies with blinders. They also must recognize the dangerous path they walk when they make an exception.

In the end, reader comments are the most honest evaluation of our work. A newspaper void of reader interaction is a newspaper of little value.

The worst mistake an editor can make is to act like God. That happens when an editor fails to listen to his or her readers and assumes there's only one right answer to a question. This book is an attempt to explain how the editor/reader relationship is a partnership, but one in which the reader has final say.

My tenure as editor was truly an invigorating experience, due to my connection with readers. The kinship was not always rosy, however; overseeing a small-town newspaper can be a lonely job, as decisions are regularly second-guessed. The same story can energize or dismay readers, depending on their relationship to and perspective on the report.

Editors routinely hold their breath in anticipation of reader reaction following in-depth reports that culminate weeks-long investigations. Those reports are typically prepared, reviewed and scrutinized again with painstaking care.

The reality is that the everyday decisions — and resulting reports — in small-town newsrooms usually generate the greatest reader reaction. Why isn't a family permitted to include in a birth announcement all grandparents and brothers and sisters of the newborn? Why can't a youth sports team expect to receive the same coverage as a varsity squad? Why won't the newspaper regularly publish columns from civic clubs?

These decisions, and many others, rarely are easy. But editors will be in a stronger position with readers if their decisions are guided by policies that emphasize fairness and consistency.

This book underscores that there is a place — in fact, a need — for community newspapers to remain aggressive in their reporting. That is at the core of editors earning the respect of their readers. But that aggressiveness must be paired with a respect for the people being covered, and an understanding of how articles affect them.

Chapter 1

Foundation of the community press

Star athletes expect to read their names in the local newspaper after scoring three touchdowns or making a game-winning basket. But imagine the surprise — to them and their parents — when the community reads about an athlete's suspension for violating state high school league rules.

Photos also can be a shock. While all editors love to feature hometown pride, the reaction can be quite different when the page-one photo is the scene of a fatal accident involving a local resident.

Community newspapers need to print all the news — the good and the bad, but especially the sensitive and tough news — if they are to remain relevant. Covering these types of stories will ensure that the community press remains vital — that readers will continue to pick up the next edition.

It's a safe bet that most newspapers have been asked to announce the grand opening of a business. But how many business owners have initiated coverage of major layoffs or a closing? Are both items of equal news value?

How many editors would expect to be approached to publicize that a local sheriff's employee was named national corrections officer of the year? How many editors would expect to be notified if county officials placed their top jail administrator on leave for alleged violation of personnel policy? Are both items of equal news value?

Both scenarios occurred at the *Red Wing Republican Eagle*. All the stories — the good and bad news — were pursued and reported in detail. But, as one might expect, the "good" news was eagerly delivered to the newspaper staff, while the newspaper received the "bad" news secondhand through confidential tips.

Community newspapers must be prepared to print all the news if they are to survive. Local news includes stories that people like to read, and stories that may not be so welcome but are just as important.

Each year the community press is challenged for its market share as individuals turn to a variety of avenues for news. But no one is in a better position to report local news than writers in small-town newspapers — individuals who live, work and play on a daily basis with their readers.

Every editor can list the principal news elements that are key to vibrant community newspapers — coverage of schools and sports, reports on government decision-makers, features on civic clubs that add to local quality of life. But what about the sensitive stories? Those are equally important to communities, but are not so readily reported.

Consider these examples:

A high school basketball team was ranked among the top teams in the state. It was cruising along in first place, then got dumped unexpectedly by a lower-tier team. How did it happen? Two starters did not play — one was on a college recruiting trip and the other was disciplined for fighting.

A city dump truck collided with a motorcyclist, killing the cyclist. A clearly distraught truck driver crouched at the scene, consoled by a passer-by. The newspaper's photographer happened to pass the scene, capturing the full emotions in a photo.

An elementary-school boy committed suicide, apparently the result of excessive ribbing by classmates. The aftermath of the suicide lingered in the school.

All three incidents have common elements: They're being talked about in the community. They have an impact on people beyond the individuals involved. They're sensitive issues.

The overriding point, however, is that all three are news. They must be reported if community newspapers truly are to be recorders of living history.

Sensitive issues discussed in this book have another common element. Many people often view the "news" as an invasion of privacy. That can complicate getting a story and having it accepted by readers.

Take the example of a city's top economic development official who was fired by the board of directors. The dismissal opened the city to a lawsuit, raised questions about the viability of the agency, and placed a cloud over the integrity of the official. The person's performance was examined at a public meeting.

In contrast, consider a star basketball player suspended for two games. His absence increased the odds that the team's winning streak would be snapped, threatened the team's state ranking, and tarnished the athlete's character in the eyes of many players and fans.

Newspapers ought to be reporting both stories, but there is a key difference in the case of the suspended athlete. Many state laws prevent school officials from releasing any information about player discipline — even their names. Doing so may even subject school representatives to civil penalties.

But that should not be a reason for newspapers to avoid the story. From a practical standpoint, news of the athlete had circulated by word of mouth. More important, though, newspapers have a responsibility to report the facts. They have just as much an obligation to report the factors leading to a team's loss as they do to report the circumstances behind a city agency not performing up to par.

No doubt, it's much easier for big-city newspapers to report these stories. Editors and reporters are nameless and faceless among most readers. A story of a suspended athlete may be the only time a reporter has contact with a particular team or school. The story, though it creates a stir, is only one among a multitude of items in a metropolitan newspaper. Any protest — a threat to drop advertising or to encourage people to cancel their subscriptions — will have minimal financial ramifications.

Contrast that with circumstances facing small-town newsrooms. Editors and reporters are well known; many people identify them as "the newspaper." Sports reporters are practically team members; they are at most every game and know players and coaches on a first-name basis. The identification of a suspended athlete will be noticed. Any hint that newspapers could lose a major advertiser or a significant number of subscriptions will draw publishers' attention and possibly intervention.

The very elements that place small-town reporters in difficult predicaments also are the exact reasons they are in optimal position for writing about sensitive issues. Reporters may have personal connections, a friend or relative to the individuals involved. They might visualize themselves as the subject of a story.

The close relationship between community newspapers and the people they serve also can prove a hindrance, though. Residents will be quick to call editors, wondering why a particular item went unreported. Some of the same readers simultaneously will cry sensationalism for reporting that puts them in an unflattering light.

Sensationalism is a longstanding criticism of newspapers and was affirmed by the American Society of Newspaper Editors' Credibility Project. The report, first published in 1999, identified and addressed the root causes of journalism's dwindling credibility. Among the six major findings: "The public believes that newspapers chase and overcover sensational stories, because they're exciting and they sell papers. They don't believe these stories deserve the attention and play they get."

The finding is not surprising. In fact, many small-town editors probably agree and are quick to make a distinction between their conduct and the conduct of their metropolitan counterparts. They need only recall the last time a story in their own back yard drew statewide attention and big-city media flocked to their towns.

The research does have important lessons for community journalists, however. For instance, the ASNE study reported that 73 percent of the public believes "newspapers should not publish a news story if they can only reach one side for comment." That's basic in the pursuit of any story, but especially those involving challenging circumstances.

A project of the Free Press/Fair Press Project of The Freedom Forum in Arlington, Va., provides additional guidance. The research resulted in a handbook, "Best Practices for Newspaper Journalists," written by Robert J. Haiman, president emeritus and distinguished editor in residence at the Poynter Institute in St. Petersburg, Fla.

The handbook was a result of conversations with the public during 1998-99 and identified nine reasons why the public thinks newspapers are unfair:

■ They get the facts wrong. The frequency of errors — spelling and grammatical errors, wrong names, wrong titles, wrong addresses, wrong dates and other similar mistakes — is a major reason why the public is increasingly skeptical of what it reads.

■ They refuse to admit errors. There is a broad feeling that newspapers not only make too many mistakes, but that they also are unwilling to correct them fully and promptly.

■ They won't name names. The distaste for anonymous sources was reflected in the ASNE credibility study. In that survey, 77 percent of respondents said they were "somewhat" (49 percent) or "very" (28 percent) concerned about the credibility of a story that contained unidentified sources.

■ They have ignorant or incompetent reporters. Business, community and civic leaders say they and their organizations often are covered by reporters who simply do not know enough about the subjects they are trying to report.

■ They prey on the weak. The public believes the press often takes unfair advantage of people who are suddenly and unexpectedly thrust into the news and unprepared to deal with questioning by reporters.

■ They concentrate on bad news. The concern that the press focuses too much on what is wrong, violent and bizarre, and that it never prints "good news," may be the longest-running complaint.

■ They lack diversity. The American press has come a long way in the last 30 years in an effort to create newspapers that reflect their communities more fully and fairly, but the public believes much work remains in both newspaper employment and content.

■ They allow editorial bias in news stories. The most powerful concern about bias raised in roundtables was the perception that news organizations had a "negative" bias.

■ They can't admit that sometimes there's no story. Several elected and appointed office-holders in roundtables expressed frustration with reporters who seem absolutely convinced — at the very beginning of the reporting process and long before all bases have been touched — that their story is going to be a blockbuster.

Reporting the challenging stories necessarily involves ethical decisions. Many professional codes guide the work of journalists. Examples include those written by the Society of Professional Journalists, National Press Photographers Association and National Conference of Editorial Writers.

Ethics dictate that reporters approach these stories in a manner sensitive to the people involved. Ethics dictate fair and consistent coverage. Ethics dictate that news policies be well thought out and flexible enough to permit exceptions, when warranted. Ethics dictate that newspapers be responsible and accountable to their readers, and ready and willing to admit "we were wrong."

At the same time, adherence to ethical reporting should not negate aggressive reporting and, specifically, should not discourage printing stories viewed as unwelcome or disturbing to readers. Newspapers have an obligation and responsibility to report all the news.

Community newspapers walk a delicate path as one of the few remaining institutions governed by ethics and relevancy. It's incumbent that small-town editors and publishers preserve that bastion. The community press is a rich part of this nation's heritage and culture and yet is not understood by many people.

To that end, developing policies and then educating readers on how newsrooms operate is vitally important to newspapers' continued livelihood.

It's necessary again to reinforce the distinction between small-market and big-market newspapers. Small-town newspapers are not immune to such things as staff turnover or out-of-town ownership — ingredients that can lead to a disconnect between newspapers and readers. But, as a general rule, reporters in small towns identify better with their communities.

The *Red Wing Republican Eagle* prided itself in aggressive reporting of local news. Guidelines set forth in this book are not an attempt to convince editors that one newspaper's approach is the right way or only way. But it's imperative that newsrooms have the conversation about why it's important to tackle tough issues.

Editors will learn some procedures for developing news policies. That is only part of the equation. Policies are of little good if reporters can't get the information — facts not always readily available, or at least not willingly offered through routine news channels.

Newspapers also will get tips on how to explain news decisions to readers. Or, in some cases, it may be necessary for editors and reporters to state their cases within their own organizations. Witness an episode shared by Hal Tarleton, editor of *The Wilson Daily Times*, a newspaper of 16,500 circulation in North Carolina.

The story involved the death of a leading business executive who founded a paving and construction company. About 15 years earlier, he had been involved in a statewide fraud case involving collusion among paving companies in contract bids. He and several other executives were convicted and spent time in federal prison.

"He never talked to us about the case before or after his conviction, but, of course, it was front-page news," Tarleton said. "His death was also front-page news, and I wanted to include his fraud conviction, along with all of his accomplishments and accolades. A two-sentence mention of the conviction ran at the end of the story, on the jump page."

The newspaper was inundated with complaints, and many people can-

What is local news?

The American Society of Newspaper Editors, through its Readership Issues Committee, published "The Local News Handbook" in 1999, in which it identified 10 dimensions of local news:

■ Proximity. The closer news is to readers, the greater the interest.

■ Safety. People must feel safe in their homes and neighborhoods; crime news has been a mainstay of newspaper content.

■ Utility. Newspapers should provide information helpful in people's daily lives.

■ Government. Intense coverage of local government is at the heart of community newspapers' missions, but it must be relevant to readers and encourage citizen participation.

■ Education. Schools have a large place in the hearts and minds of citizens, and newspapers must cover them well.

■ Spirituality. People seek others who share their beliefs and, in fact, many more people attend weekend worship services than sports events. Remember that when planning your religion pages.

■ Support. Americans participate in a wide and rapidly growing variety of support groups.

■ Identity. People want to feel they are part of a community.

■ Recognition. Never underestimate the importance of getting people's names in print, even if it's in six-point type in a scoreboard.

■ Empowerment. Community is defined by collective action on common concerns of life, and newspapers facilitate that.

celed their subscriptions. "I told people who called me that when Nixon died (he was still alive at the time), Watergate would certainly be a part of his obit," Tarleton said.

How did the newspaper respond? Tarleton reported that his publisher wrote an editorial — the first he'd ever written — "more or less apologizing and extolling the businessman's many virtues." Tarleton said he still thinks the reporting was fair and reasonable in including the federal conviction in the obituary, but in retrospect, he's not sure it was worth all the flak the newspaper received.

Tarleton was correct in his approach to the story. But the example offers an important reminder that all departments — including management — must be involved in developing or at least being aware of policies for handling sensitive stories. Or, in the North Carolina example, the publisher might have been consulted about including the two sentences of sensitive information. Publishers are likely to support reporting the sensitive stories if they are involved in formulating policies and are informed of stories that have the potential of drawing reader criticism.

The most important lesson, however, is that newsrooms understand the importance of consistency and fairness in reporting any story, especially those involving sensitive and challenging circumstances. Readers may disagree with policies, but they will be even less forgiving if newspapers exercise double standards.

Chapter 2
Developing a policy and making it known

Making the right decisions regarding sensitive stories is easier if you have policies in place. Elements of sound policies for reporting sensitive issues are similar to the elements of solid news stories. The same questions should be asked and the same avenues pursued:

■ Who should participate in developing policies?
■ What should be reported?
■ Where should a story be displayed?
■ When should a story be published?
■ Why is it a story?
■ How should policies be communicated?

Who should participate in developing policies?

The newspaper office is an excellent beginning point, and that doesn't mean soliciting ideas from reporters only. Include staff from circulation, composing, advertising, pressroom and the business office. Talk to carriers and motor route drivers. The circle of knowledge in developing policies is much broader than the collective mind of a newsroom. Newspaper employees and, by extension, their families and friends, bring to the table a diversity of backgrounds and experiences. In many instances, their values — their perspectives on how stories should be reported — can be a barometer of community values.

Newspaper employees represent the first tier of contacts when forming any policy — whether it pertains to items as routine as wedding and engagement announcements and obituaries, or more challenging topics such as business layoffs and suspended high school athletes. Then there's a vast second tier of people. The individuals will vary, depending on the subject. Contacts should include those people directly affected by a policy, and others who may have a special perspective.

For example, if newspapers are considering identifying names of suspended high school athletes, editors and reporters should talk with school officials — from the superintendent to principals to coaches. Most school boards have liaisons to a high school league or other body that governs alcohol and drug use by athletes. Visit with sports booster clubs. Get reactions from athletes who have been suspended but whose discipline went unreported.

It is equally vital to touch base with an informal network of individuals. Where are people likely to talk about the exploits — good and bad —

of their hometown teams? Coffee shops and barber shops are good bets. And don't forget the fans who attend sporting events long after their children and grandchildren have graduated.

Many people can be helpful in each step, from development to implementation of a policy. Editors also must recognize that in the end, few policies will win unanimous approval. But readers will be more understanding if they realize newspapers have followed a procedure and strived to talk to as many people as possible.

Solicitation of opinions must be genuine. Editors also must be square with people that, in the end, the parameters of a policy will be a newspaper decision.

Editors will receive feedback naturally from those who disagree with how news items are handled. It's part of the everyday give-and-take with readers. But newspapers must initiate meetings to gain people's and groups' perspectives on the development of policies. In some instances, editors can talk to individuals one-on-one. In other cases, editors might request to meet with a group, such as a quarterly meeting of high school sports coaches. Or newspapers might regularly convene "brown bag" lunches, inviting a cross-section of readers to discuss various newsroom practices and policies.

Newspapers foremost must talk to as many people as possible in developing policies. It's equally important, however, to occasionally reconnect with people and organizations to see if changing circumstances dictate that policies be revised.

What should be reported?

Newsrooms must strive to treat similar events in a similar manner. Consistency shows readers that decisions are made fairly and not arbitrarily. Consistency, however, does not mean that each instance of a particular type of story is reported the same. Suicides are an excellent example. Newspapers may decide to report them, but only if they meet certain criteria. Did the death involve a public official? Did the death occur in a public setting? Did the death prompt an investigation?

Answers are not always clear cut. Regarding a policy for suicides, what is the definition of public officials — elected and/or appointed individuals? Do city, county and school department heads fall into that category? What about midlevel managers, and how are they defined? Are presidents of major local companies considered public figures — if not according to the letter of the law, at least the spirit of the law?

Also muddying the picture is the ability to get information. There may be universal agreement about what to report, but information is not always readily available. Indeed, certain facts may be classified as private under state laws. Reporters often have other channels to get the information, but they may not be able to track it down in all instances.

Where should a story be displayed?

This question, like many of the others, does not have a "one size fits all" answer. Some sensitive stories always deserve front-page coverage, and others should be relegated to the inside.

Significance is a primary factor, just as it is in deciding the position of any story. Editors need to pause a moment when reporting on sensitive issues. In many cases, word already has spread, and readers will be anticipating a newspaper report. Furthermore, community papers are normally thoroughly read, so placing a sensitive story on an inside page may not reduce its readership.

Newspapers will win points from readers by avoiding the shock treatment of splashing a story on the front page. Sensitive stories demand sensitivity to placement.

When should a story be published?

Stories usually are reported as soon as all the facts are gathered. Timing is a special consideration when tackling sensitive issues, however.

Newspapers often fall short of the mark in reporting the everyday public records, and editors often underestimate the impact of delayed reports. Consider a couple who went through a turbulent divorce and wants to put it behind them. The divorce, even though it's a single line in the paper, is reported six weeks after the papers are signed.

Consider a family that has gone through the painful process of bankruptcy. They've finally accepted and reconciled their predicament and are facing the future with a positive attitude. The newspaper carries the notice three months after the fact, prompting a new round of calls from creditors.

The impact of postponed reports on sensitive stories can take an even greater toll on individuals involved. Consider parents who have lost a child to suicide, and then suffer new anguish when the newspaper reports the cause of death two days after the funeral.

Untimely reports also can make newspapers look downright foolish. A newspaper picks up a tip that an athlete was suspended for two games. Standing on the principle that it is a newspaper of record, the sports staff reports the suspension — even though the player has been back in action for two games.

Deciding when to publish sensitive stories warrants examination beyond that given to routine stories. Policies must allow flexibility for less than optimal conditions — for example, when a desire for a timely report is hindered by an inability to get all the facts. Which takes precedence? When faced with such a predicament, it is helpful to convene a meeting to evaluate the pros and cons of publishing or holding a story.

Newspapers often have legitimate reasons for delaying reports, especially in the realm of public records. Court papers may not be processed for days or even weeks after disposition of cases. Editors and reporters cannot expect readers to know of these inherent postponements. Explaining the reasons to readers leads to the "why" and "how" of developing policies.

Why is it a story?

Local news is the franchise of community newspapers. That includes good news, bad news, sensitive news and everything in between.

Not all readers subscribe to that theory, as documented by a wealth of research. Small-town editors don't need surveys to learn the pulse of communities. Readers are unafraid to tell editors directly when they believe stories are out of bounds.

Newsrooms post a list of "dos" and "don'ts" for almost everything that gets published. If newspapers have guidelines for what constitutes business news, they also should state with clarity the parameters for reporting on tough and sensitive issues.

This is another time when it is helpful to involve as many people as reasonable. Visit with people who are directly involved in an issue. For example, what do grief counselors think of publication of photos from a fatal accident scene? Talk to regular readers, too.

Consider all perspectives of why a story should be pursued. In the case of a fatal accident, will a story and/or photo draw attention to a community problem, such as the growing numbers of youths who are ticketed for drinking and driving? Will a story spur citizen action, such as a petition to install traffic signals at a particularly dangerous intersection?

The nature of sensitive stories places an even greater burden on newspapers to explain decisions. Policies also should be reviewed regularly to see if they need rethinking in light of changing circumstances.

How should policies be communicated?

Newspapers constantly promote their pages as the best avenue for businesses, organizations, institutions and individuals to deliver messages. A landfill is changing its hours of operation. A store is carrying a new product. An individual is having a garage sale. What better place to spread the word than in the local newspaper?

Yet newspapers remain among the worst at notifying readers of changes in their own operations. The "why" of reporting on sensitive issues warrants attention. The more people who are aware of a change, the smoother the implementation.

It's an easy process to notify people and organizations directly affected by new policies by sending them notices. Personal phone calls or face-to-face meetings are recommended if editors expect resistance or pointed questions.

In the end, however, newspapers must inform readers, the people who ultimately will be most affected and the ones who may not find out about changes until too late. It does little good to announce new deadlines for engagement and wedding announcements only on the written forms. The deadline may have already passed when a couple picks up a form.

Newspapers should convey guidelines and policies on a regular basis, whether via house ads or messages from the publisher or editor. Some policies cannot be reinforced enough. Among the many examples are deadlines for news items and guidelines for letters to the editor.

Newspapers also must be sensitive to how and when they explain these policies.

A barrage of complaints — especially if they are published as letters to the editor — about the treatment of someone can put editors in a predicament. Any attempt to defend, or explain, a story also places attention on the very subject, or victims, of a story about which readers are complaining. On the other hand, if editors do not respond, newspapers will be charged with being unsympathetic.

What does this all mean?

Newspapers can go to great lengths to develop all sorts of policies, and they still will be caught flat-footed on occasion. News occurs 24 hours a day, seven days a week. Deadlines and other circumstances do not always allow newsrooms to refer to their ABCs of reporting sensitive issues, and then proceed in an orderly fashion. Even the most comprehensive written policies are certain to miss some circumstances.

Another element — discussion — is common to all of these steps in developing policies. All decisions are stronger if the options are talked about with as many individuals as possible — people within and outside of the newsroom. Discussions don't mean consensus will be developed, but it assures that editors will get many perspectives before making a final call.

Chapter 3
Reporting suicides

Youth found dead near home

Joe Smith, 13, son of Jeremy and Susan Smith, was found dead at 12:30 p.m. Saturday outdoors, on land near his home.

Dr. Ted Rollins, county coroner, said the cause of death was hanging. As of this morning, he had not ruled whether it was accidental or suicide. The incident remains under investigation.

Suicide reports stir strong emotions from family and friends. The stories prompt strident complaints that newspapers are invading personal affairs. Newspapers also face strong resistance from authorities about releasing information, even though cause of death is public information under many state laws.

The incidence of suicide — it was the No. 3 cause of death among people ages 15 to 24, according to a U.S. surgeon general's report in 1997 — is why the topic deserves examination as a broader social concern. But the growing death count doesn't make the reporting of suicide any easier for newspapers, especially in small towns.

A suicide in Red Wing, Minn., offered an opportunity for community-wide discussion, but it required a great deal of care by the newspaper staff, coordination with professionals, and extraordinary cooperation by the family.

Developing the policy

Consistency and fairness are especially important considerations when reporting suicides.

Even newspapers that reject the idea of reporting suicides cannot ignore that some circumstances demand an exception. For example, an individual tied up traffic on a high bridge before jumping to his death. Police officers surrounded a house where someone was holding hostages at gunpoint; the person committed suicide rather than surrendering. An elected official — the mayor — took his own life.

Many newspapers adopt a policy to report suicides only if they involve public officials or if they occur in public settings. The three previous examples fit into those categories. But the definition of what is a public or private setting, or who is a public or private individual, is not always so clear.

Think about the following scenarios:

A bank president who has served on numerous community boards is found dead in a car in a city parking lot. What if the same man commits suicide at home? Reflect on those circumstances, but now substitute a retail clerk as the suicide victim.

A star athlete is found dead outside school as students arrive for class. Then consider his discovery late at night by a janitor. Reflect on the same circumstances, but now substitute a student who isn't involved in any extracurricular activities as the suicide victim.

Mayors are public officials. Newspapers are in an excellent position to defend reporting a mayor's suicide. But are bank presidents, or other major business figures in small communities, any less noteworthy?

Newspapers frequently are challenged about whether it's fair to families — just because they have been determined prominent under someone's objective or subjective guidelines — that their personal tragedies, or successes, get publicized.

Editors must view that situation from the opposite perspective. By not reporting a suicide — because an individual has not been deemed important — is that sending a message that a family's loss is less important?

Among questions to consider when establishing guidelines:

■ When do suicides warrant front-page coverage?

■ How much detail should be included? Should the cause of death be identified — i.e. asphyxiation, drug overdose, gunshot or knife wound?

■ Should photos of the individuals ever accompany a story?

■ Should suicides of former residents be reported? What are the parameters?

■ Should the names of survivors of a victim be mentioned in a news story, especially if the individuals are prominent?

■ Should suicide be reported as the cause of death in an obituary?

As with the development of any policy, it's important to talk with certain individuals in framing suicide coverage.

Health-care professionals should be among the first contacts. Talk to school counselors, mental health advocates, clergy, law enforcement personnel and medical response teams. Ask to speak at a meeting of grief support groups.

Don't forget that co-workers at newspapers may be among the best resources. They and their families are community members, too.

Implementing the policy

One principle is for newspapers to record all deaths that are the result of unnatural causes. Suicide falls into this category, but is different from accidents, drownings or homicides. Many people point out that suicide is the result of depression, a sickness.

It's also a good practice to report suicides in stories separate from obituaries, recognizing that families often keep obituaries as permanent remembrances of the deceased.

Newsrooms have a responsibility to address the link between depression and suicide if they want to be a positive force in addressing suicide as a social concern. In that regard, reporting a suicide is just the first step. Follow-up stories are equally, if not more, important.

Several angles can be pursued:

■ What are the causes of suicide?

■ What are the recent advances in prevention?

■ What are the warning signs of depression and suicide?

■ What are the myths of suicide?

■ Are local agencies, support groups and hot lines available to people contemplating suicide?

■ What should people do if they suspect someone is considering suicide?

■ Are response teams in place for dealing with the aftermath of suicide?

■ What are the trends in suicide rates?

Consider stories about individuals who overcame despair without

Don't encourage copycat suicides

Newspapers can be a positive force in educating people about suicide prevention, but they can also exacerbate a bad situation, according to a report, "Reporting on Suicide: Recommendations for the Media."

Chief authors of the 2001 report were the American Association for Suicide Prevention, American Association of Suicidology and Annenberg Public Policy Center. The research underscores the link between suicide and mental illness and reinforces that guidelines for reporting suicides must include coverage of the death as well as follow-up stories.

The study cautions that certain ways of describing suicide contribute to what behavioral scientists call copycat suicides. For example:

■ Research suggests that inadvertently romanticizing suicide or idealizing those who take their own lives by portraying suicide as a heroic or romantic act may encourage others to identify with the victim.

■ Exposure to methods of suicide through media reports can encourage vulnerable individuals to imitate them. Research indicates that detailed descriptions or pictures of the location of a suicide encourage attempting suicide.

These all can be worthwhile and educational stories. But newspapers must consider the impact on victims' families and friends. No matter how the stories are pursued and presented, a personal tragedy is the spring-board for the coverage. Follow-up stories, no matter how well intentioned, will put a family back in the spotlight.

Sometimes, though, families are the newspaper's best allies. One family in Red Wing decided to go public and created a positive environment for the community to discuss a problem more widespread than most people wanted to acknowledge.

A 19-year-old was found dead in his home. The death was especially painful as it was the second son this family had lost. The victim's brother had died five years earlier in a car accident.

The suicide prompted an early morning phone call to the editor from mental health counselors. The death occurred during the summer, and there was no easy way for counselors to connect with students. A notice was put in the newspaper inviting friends to a meeting that evening.

But counselors wanted to go a step further. This youth suffered from depression — he had never gotten over his brother's death — and coun-selors requested a story on depression and the signs of suicide. A sidebar would list agencies and hot lines for individuals to contact.

Community newspapers should do these stories. In this case, howev-

imitation.

■ Presenting suicide as the inexplicable act of an otherwise healthy or high-achieving person may encourage identification with the victim.

The most thoughtful policies will prove of little value unless editors and reporters take the same care in writing and displaying the actual sto-ries. In the case of suicide, that means giving attention to specific words in headlines and text.

In this regard, the report recommends:

■ Whenever possible, it is preferable to avoid referring to suicide in a headline. Unless the death took place in public, the cause of death should be reported in the body of the story and not in the headline.

■ In the body of the story, it is preferable to describe the deceased as "having died by suicide," rather than as "a suicide," or having "commit-ted suicide." The latter two expressions reduce the person to the mode of death, or connote criminal or sinful behavior.

■ Contrasting "suicide deaths" with "non-fatal attempts" is prefer-able to using terms such as "successful," "unsuccessful" or "failed."

er, the timing and sensitivity to the family were priorities. The editor balked at proceeding unless the family was comfortable with the coverage.

The outcome turned out to be beneficial to everyone. The counselor acted as the initial liaison. The result was a front-page story in which family members shared their son's struggles with depression. The story appeared prior to the funeral and helped ease the tension among family members and visitors.

The interview was also the start of a broader community response. The family worked with a mental health center to sponsor a forum to help people understand the dynamics of depression and suicide. An overflow crowd filled a theater to hear personal stories from panelists, including local residents. Crisis hot lines were immediately flooded with calls.

A local bank took note of the response and decided to take the discussion to another level. Bank personnel met with the family, and a steering committee was formed with representatives from school, youth and health-care professionals. Within a few months the bank, assisted by a private foundation, brought the founders of the Light for Life Foundation International-Yellow Ribbon Suicide Prevention Program to the community. The national project was started by parents of a suicide victim in Westminster, Colo.

The steering committee, working with mental-health professionals, conducted school assemblies for each of grades 7 to 12. Counselors were available to talk. Between the middle school and high school, approximately 60 kids came forward for immediate counseling. Nearly 150 kids volunteered to work on creating a youth board.

The steering committee also succeeded in getting the school to include discussion of depression and suicide in the health curriculum beginning in eighth grade.

Not all suicides will have such an impact. Not all families of victims will be so sharing of a tragedy. The underlying lesson, however, is that even issues as sensitive as suicide can become a positive force in communities if newspapers treat the subject with respect and care.

Explaining the policy

Newspapers do well to explain their policies to readers as quickly as possible after the fact, especially if someone raises a question. In most instances, explanations can be readily delivered. However, a direct explanation is not so easy, and may not be the best practice, when discussing suicide coverage. Families already are grieving, and circumstances are exacerbated by the fact that the cause of death was suicide.

Reporting suicides

The final step in developing and implementing policies is communicating with readers. Following is Editor Jim Pumarlo's column about covering suicides in the *Red Wing Republican Eagle*:

Nothing receives greater scrutiny than the Republican Eagle's policy on the reporting of suicides.

We don't expect to change many readers' minds. But a recent report promotes the idea that it's far healthier for society to talk about — rather than hide — suicides.

U.S. Surgeon General David Satcher provides a compelling reason for public discussion on suicide and its causes. Suicide is the eighth leading cause of death in the United States, claiming 85 lives each day. Each year, half a million Americans try to kill themselves and fail, and another 30,000 succeed.

In Goodhue County, 15 percent of ninth-graders attempted suicide in 1998, according to the Children's Report Card issued this month by the Minnesota Department of Planning.

While we have serious doubts about the validity of any such statistic, the number of suicide deaths nationwide is considerably more than homicide, which claims about 19,000 lives annually. And though the death rate due to suicide has remained steady over the years, the incidence of suicide among adolescents and young adults has nearly tripled since the early 1950s. For people between ages 15 and 24, suicide is the third leading cause of death.

The numbers alone dictate that greater attention be given to suicides. But there are other reasons this newspaper acknowledges suicides.

R-E policy is to report, whenever possible, the causes of all deaths that are the result of other than natural circumstances. Suicides fall into that category along with such things as accidents, shootings and drownings.

We believe it's also healthy for families to discuss why people take their lives, especially if there have been a number of suicides in a community or if the individuals happen to be friends or relatives.

As the surgeon general's report notes, those people most vulnerable to suicide are easy to spot. They often are suffering from depression or other mood-affecting brain diseases. They might be struggling with chemical dependency, physical illness, a personal loss or social isolation.

Frank and open discussion leads to greater understanding and might well prevent similar tragedies.

The R-E takes great care in how it reports suicide. Few details are given unless there's a significant purpose for doing so — such as if it occurred in a public setting. And the information is published on a page separate from where the obituary appears.

We're sensitive to the fact that families often keep obituaries as permanent records. Therefore, we make no mention of the suicide in the obituary unless, of course, the family requests.

The sensitivity of suicide almost makes the subject taboo to bring up in general conversation, and it brings a feeling of guilt or embarrassment to mention in an obituary.

That in itself is unfortunate, because suicide truly is an epidemic. Suicide claimed nearly twice as many lives as did HIV and AIDS, according to 1997 U.S. statistics. Public and private interests have spent millions of dollars to combat those diseases.

To his credit, Satcher is proposing strategies to address suicide, too. A first step is to acknowledge and talk about suicide in our communities.

Too often the media are portrayed as sticking a microphone in people's faces and asking them to react at a time of tragedy. The story of a particular suicide shows that it is possible and far more constructive for all involved to work as partners — rather than adversaries — in writing stories about human tragedy. Here is Jim Pumarlo's follow-up column to the suicide:

Riley family shows immense courage
Aug. 22, 2002

The death of Larry Riley resonated throughout Red Wing last week.

The 19-year-old son of Doug and Diane Riley, and brother of Robin, took his own life Aug. 11. The pain was exacerbated by the fact that five years earlier his brother, Sam, was killed in a car accident.

Yet, less than three days after the death, the Rileys spoke with an R-E staff writer about their tragedy. The front-page story appeared the day of Larry's visitation, and it generated widespread, positive response.

Primary credit goes to the Rileys who were willing to share their story, and to Richard Olson and his staff at the Mental Health Center who helped us hook up with the family. It's instructive as well for readers to know the sensitivity with which we approached the story.

First contact

Representatives of the Mental Health Center made the original contact to discuss a way to share with readers — primarily friends of Larry Riley — the signs of depression and suicide. It's fairly routine for schools to bring in counselors to talk with students in the aftermath of a tragedy.

But this occurred during the summer with no organized opportunity to meet with Larry's peers. Counselors were available Monday afternoon for a brief period at the church, but the need was evident for broader distribution of the message.

The R-E's policy on suicide is often much debated — the fact that we always report the cause of death. That is our policy for reporting all deaths by other than natural causes.

Sensitive to family

It's equally important, we believe, if we can be a partner in presenting information that may prevent copycat occurrences. We were sensitive to the fact that we could not write such an article without referring to Larry Riley's death, and we did not want to run the article without the family's awareness — even blessing.

A Mental Health Center staff member, who also is a friend of the Rileys, made the contact and the family agreed to the interview.

The timing of the article played another role, too. We intentionally published it the day of the visitation with the thought that it would help friends visiting the family understand the illness that led to his death — depression. More than one person told us that they initially did not intend to go to the funeral home, but changed their minds after the article appeared.

The article prompted others to urge the R-E to do more of these kinds of stories. And we have done articles on the tendency of people to go into depression around holidays such as Christmas. But it was the circumstances — the ability to link advice from the Mental Health Center to a specific incident — that made this story so powerful.

"Suffering without meaning is a tragedy," Doug and Diane Riley said last week. We thank them for openly talking about the loss of their son and for helping people to better understand the circumstances.

Too often the media get portrayed as sticking a microphone in people's faces and asking them to react at a time of tragedy. The Larry Riley story shows it is possible and far more constructive for all involved to work as partners — rather than adversaries — in writing stories about human tragedy.

Chapter 4
Covering sexual abuse cases

Minnesota News Council

Determination 106
August 24, 1995

In the matter of a complaint of anonymous juvenile incest victim against *The Wabasha* (Minn.) *County Herald.*

A 17-year-old incest victim attended the hearing to press her complaint. Accompanying her were her mother and her therapist. Representing *The Wabasha County Herald* were Michael Smith, editor, and Gary Stumpf, publisher.

Complaint: The complainant contended that the July 12, 1995, story about her father's sentencing:

■ Invaded her privacy when it identified the victim of the sexual assaults as the convicted man's minor daughter (she was his only daughter).

■ Was sensational and revictimized the daughter by publishing graphic details of the abuse she endured.

Determination: The Minnesota News Council chose not to vote on invasion of privacy or sensationalism, but after discussion decided that the newspaper had been insensitive to the girl. Members suggested that the newspaper should have consulted others in developing the story and could have talked with the family to prepare them for the story. A council member urged the newspaper to think not only of journalistic standards, but also community standards.

The council also voted unanimously to recommend that the newspaper create guidelines for covering sexual-abuse cases, consulting with outsiders including counselors and victims.

The Minnesota News Council addresses and promotes fairness in media through public discussion. The organization offers an alternative to legal action. Complainants state their case at a hearing before a council comprised of media and public members. Media members participating in *The Wabasha County Herald* case included Jim Pumarlo, editor of the *Red Wing Republican Eagle.*

31

Sexual abuse is one of the most sensitive topics reported in newspapers. The victims often want to avoid publicity, but reporting sex crimes may help prevent future sex crimes and help victims find sources of help.

Exemplary reporters excel in their instinct to identify news and their ability to get a story, no matter how many or how difficult the obstacles. Newspapers that lack aggressive editors and reporters will become irrelevant to readers and the community.

But, reporters will gain more respect from peers and readers if they show respect for the subjects of their stories. Reporters must exercise extra caution when approaching stories involving tough and sensitive circumstances, such as sexual abuse.

A story published in July 1995 in *The Wabasha* (Minn.) *County Herald*, a weekly newspaper in a town of about 2,500 people, offers a case study of a sensitive story — and steps that should be followed from start to finish. The newspaper reported the sentencing of a father who was convicted of incest. The victim was his only daughter.

The daughter complained that the newspaper's report was insensitive, and the Minnesota News Council ruled in her favor. Though council hearings produce a winner and loser in terms of the vote, the underlying value is that everyone leaves with a better understanding and appreciation of the other's perspective.

The complaint against *The Wabasha County Herald* would likely have never reached the Minnesota News Council had the principles underscored at the hearing been practiced by the newspaper in preparing for and pursuing the story.

Reporting sexual abuse is no easy task. Newspapers must walk a delicate path of stating the extent of the crime while still protecting the identity of the victim. It becomes nearly an impossible challenge when the case involves incest — especially sexual abuse of a minor by a parent.

The News Council vote was nearly unanimous to uphold the complaint of the daughter. The vote should not be interpreted as a blanket condemnation of the newspaper, however, nor should the vote imply that the staff was callous in its decision to identify the victim as the daughter. The publisher and editor said it was a gut-wrenching decision.

Here are some questions that should be on a checklist for evaluating whether any story really is fit for publication. Many are common-sense and taken for granted in the everyday routine of newsrooms. The danger is that they can be overlooked in the rush to get a story, especially in an effort to beat the competition.

Is it news?

Newsworthiness is the ultimate litmus test. Phrased another way, what is the impact of a story?

The equation has multiple variables. For example, what is the impact of reporting a story vs. the impact of not reporting it? Will a story bring repercussions to individuals or organizations? Are those effects negative or positive, and does it matter? Is the story of interest to the broader community?

The sexual-abuse case was an example of the values that frequently collide when editors seek to balance victims' rights with a responsibility to inform. There was no doubt that reporting the father's sentencing stirred painful childhood memories for the victim. But from the editor's standpoint, the story held the individual accountable for his crime. The seriousness of the crime warranted front-page coverage, he said.

Part of the article was about the judge's apparent leniency in the punishment. Further examination, however — principally, talking to the victim — would have revealed the daughter's role in advocating a shorter sentence. The father was sentenced to one year in jail even though state guidelines recommended 13 years in prison. The father also was placed on 30 years' probation.

The story could have prompted a review of sentencing patterns in sex-abuse cases. It also could have raised the overall awareness of sexual abuse, especially if it included follow-up stories on the signs of sexual abuse and where to turn for help.

Newspapers are asked routinely to publicize "proclamations" to create awareness about subjects. Sexual Assault Awareness Month is on that list. Sexual abuse, and myriad other topics, deserve focus. But stories are much more compelling, and readers pay more attention, when stories are linked to local circumstances. The sexual-abuse sentencing could have served as a springboard.

Is it true?

Every newsroom has likely received a tip about a story that's "too good to be true" — something with all the markings of a front-page banner headline. That's reason enough to take extra steps to ensure the veracity of a call.

Errors in fact, such as a wrong time or place, are harmful to a newspaper's credibility when they show up in something as straightforward as meeting notices. Publishing misinformation about individuals involved in sensitive stories not only can damage reputations, but it could result in legal action against newspapers.

Even if it's true, should we publish it?

Editors also must ask: Just because something is true, should it be reported? In other words, must all facts be reported? The sex-abuse case offered instruction.

The editor pointed out that he printed exactly what was in court documents. His intent was to prevent sensationalism and to circumvent gossip about what had happened in the family, he said. It's fair to ask, however, whether all details were necessary for public examination.

The family brought the complaint to the News Council on the basis of two issues: identifying the child and giving excessive detail.

The descriptive narrative of charges often is the more sensitive and bigger problem when reporting from court summaries. In this case, simply reporting the charges — repeated instances of abuse during several years — would have allowed readers to deduce the victim was a family member. (But that is not always true in such circumstances. Extensive cases of abuse also have been reported between an adult and a baby sitter or neighborhood youth.)

In any case, the community still would have had a clear picture of the abhorrent circumstances had the newspaper not identified the victim as the daughter.

What if you were the subject?

Editors should insert themselves into the story. Had the *Wabasha* publisher and editor pictured themselves as the subjects when they reviewed the sex-abuse story, they may have changed the final version. There's no better test than editors putting their own names in the headline.

If editors have opportunity, they also should discuss approaches to stories with their families or other people they hold in high regard.

Did you talk with the subject of the story?

Editors should try to interview the involved parties, or at least alert them to the story. Most individuals expect to be contacted as part of the news gathering, but that does not always occur, as illustrated in the sex-abuse case. The newspaper's failure to talk to the victim directly almost certainly altered the story's presentation.

The Wabasha County Herald was quizzed by Minnesota News Council members on whether anyone talked to the family or consulted with others prior to publication. The editor and publisher said they spoke to each other and to the prosecutor, who had urged full disclosure. They did not talk to the family or a mental health therapist, and they did not seek a woman's perspective. The editor said he had all the information and only a weekend to write the story.

In hindsight, as revealed at the News Council hearing, the decision to rely only on the county prosecutor and not contact the victim resulted in a significant omission in the story. The victim herself had asked that her father be given a lenient sentence so, in her words, her family could be reunited and try to get back to living a normal life.

The newspaper may have had only a few days to sort through the court appearance and sentencing, but the staff had months to sort through questions and prepare the coverage. As a News Council member pointed out, the father had been charged with the crime a year earlier.

Editors may even consider sharing a story in advance with key participants. Many journalists reject the idea of letting someone preview a story, and for good reason. The practice can result in problems, not the least of which is setting a precedent. But sometimes pre-publication review — with explicit ground rules established in advance — can head off serious problems.

Reviewing a story with the individuals involved does not assure that everyone will leave the room on the same page. However, it's likely that all parties in the sex-abuse case — the victim, the community and the newspaper — would have been served better had a discussion occurred.

How will you justify a decision?

Too often when readers complain about a story, editors respond, "Sorry, but that's our policy."

Policies are necessary, but they must be defensible in easy-to-understand terms. Who determined the policies? When were they last reviewed? Have circumstances changed?

The publisher and the editor of The Wabasha County Herald acknowledged that the sex-abuse story forced some difficult decisions, but they really only talked with each other. They missed an opportunity to explain to the family their approach to the story. Had they done so, they would have discovered the victim's role and reason in asking for a lenient sentence. The feedback may well have changed how the newspaper approached the story. And the editor would have had a ready-made column to explain the steps involved in presenting the case.

Is the report fair?

Stories may be factual, but does that guarantee balance? Omission of certain information, or failure to get a response from a party, can put a completely different slant on a story.

Newspapers often are criticized for lack of balance in crime and court news. It's easy to produce a story from a police report or criminal complaint. Getting a comment from the accused is not as easy. If a response is tracked down, comments often are tacked on the end of a story and appear almost as an after-thought.

The sex-abuse report was such a case. The story may have fulfilled expectations of the prosecutor, but few others. In fact, the victim — who was represented by the prosecutor — was most upset by the coverage. In a story as important as this one, including the comments of others would have produced a stronger and more accurate story.

Editors also should seek institutional memory when reporting sensitive issues. Has the newspaper ever confronted such a story before? How were circumstances handled? Readers have long memories and will be on watch to make sure newspapers stick to their standards.

Lastly, don't be afraid to admit an error in judgment or a mistake. It's the right thing to do, and it goes a long way toward restoring credibility.

Is it a public or strictly private issue?

The Wabasha County Herald and the victim agreed that the story was important.

The editor said he believed that by fully reporting the incest, the newspaper would discourage others from committing the crime for fear of publicity. He also said the newspaper had been sensitive to the well-being of the girl by choosing not to run a story when her father was first charged with the crime a year before sentencing.

The girl, who said she first wanted to keep the case secret, said she decided she wanted to help others.

The differences, of course, surfaced in how the story was reported.

The impact of such stories on victims cannot be overstated, as pointed out by Dr. Frank Ochberg, a psychiatrist and adjunct professor who helped launch and sustain the Victims and the Media Program at Michigan State University's School of Journalism. "Victims in our society already feel that they have been labeled as losers, weak and pathetic, so when you add the stigma of sexual assault, it is easy to see how vulnerable this makes them," says Ochberg, an expert on posttraumatic stress disorder who has treated many victims.

Most newspapers have policies that protect the identity of victims, but that can become difficult in small towns where word spreads quickly. Community newspapers still should make the effort.

Will the story make a difference?

The Wabasha County Herald and the victim agreed — or at least had hoped to agree — on this point, too. The editor said the publicity given the perpetrator would deter others from carrying out a similar crime. And the victim said she hoped the publicity would help others who might be in similar situations.

Newspapers must give equal attention to how a story will affect those directly involved as well as the good provided to the broader community.

An equally large part of the sex-abuse story was the reason the judge handed down a punishment far less than that recommended by sentencing guidelines. It can be argued that residents needed to know it was an incest case to put the county attorney's comments in context and to hold everyone in the criminal justice system accountable. But even to that point, the story identified the case as first-degree criminal sexual conduct, which in itself underscores the severity.

Will the truth quash rumors?

Stories report facts. At the same time, they serve to dispel myths and innuendoes. The opportunity to quash rumors is one of the strongest arguments editors can present to an otherwise unwilling or uncooperative news source.

If a rumor has reached the newspaper, rest assured it has circulated throughout the community. What better avenue is there for someone to set the record straight than to use the local newspaper? It's also the responsible thing for newspapers to do.

One word of caution, though. Rumors are neverending, especially in small towns. Editors must establish that a particular rumor is significant enough to warrant a story.

Sex-abuse reports are especially problematic. *The Wabasha County Herald* believed the story would put rumors to rest. Even the victim's therapist in this case encouraged newspapers to bring the problem to public attention.

Does a story meet journalistic and community standards?

All newspapers strive to protect victims, but it is not always possible. Consider these three cases, which all occurred during the span of a few months at the *Red Wing Republican Eagle*:

■ A defendant, in what the judge characterized as a highly unusual request, asked for a three-hour furlough from jail once a week to visit with his daughter, the victim. It was difficult to report the court proceedings without identifying — but not actually naming — the daughter.

■ A father was on trial for alleged sex abuse, but his attorney claimed what really was at issue was a custody battle between parents. The mother and daughter, the alleged victims, lived an hour away from Red Wing.

■ A father was sentenced for sexual abuse that occurred during the course of 15 years. The newspaper identified the victim as a son, since he no longer lived in Minnesota. At an attorney's suggestion, the story also made it clear the abuse did not involve children who still lived in the area.

The Minnesota News Council took two actions on the complaint against *The Wabasha County Herald*. One was to uphold the victim's complaint. The council also urged the newspaper to consult others, including sex-abuse therapists, to develop a policy for covering such sensitive stories.

That's sound advice for any newsroom. The policy may not be black and white, but it will give the newspaper a basis for making sensitive decisions that still serve the need of informing readers.

Tips for interviewing victims

The Wabasha County Herald misfired by not contacting the victim for comments in the story on the sexual-abuse sentencing.

Reporters often are as uncomfortable during a victim interview as the victim is, say Bonnie Bucqueroux and William Cote at Michigan State University's School of Journalism. Bucqueroux is coordinator of the school's Victims and the Media Program; Cote is co-chairman of the Faculty Advisory Committee for the program.

They offer the following tips for interviewing victims, especially for victims of sexual assault:

■ Grant victims a sense of power and control. Remember that victims of violence and their family and friends are suffering from horrific stress that has robbed them of their sense of mastery.

■ Discuss ground rules up front. Some have suggested, only half-jokingly, that reporters should be forced to read a version of the Miranda warning — "You have a right to remain silent ... ." While some might wince at the thought, ambush tactics have no place in a victim interview, and experience confirms that discussing issues of privacy and confidentiality at the beginning can prevent misunderstandings and problems later.

■ Prepare for the possibility that you will be the first to deliver the bad news. Reporters often telephone or appear on a family's porch looking for quotes about someone who has been killed or maimed, only to find out that no family members have yet been informed.

■ Ask permission. This is particularly important when approaching a victim's physical zone of intimacy.

■ Tips on what to say: To journalists' ears, the phrase, "Sorry for your loss," may sound trite and artificial. But it is far better to use a canned phrase that strikes the right note than the wrong words that wound.

■ Tips on what not to say: Never say, "I know how you feel." You don't, even if you think you may have suffered a similar victimization.

■ Accuracy above all. Accuracy is the overarching goal in all reporting, but the stakes are much higher here.

■ Be especially sensitive to imputations of blame. Fortunately, we have come a long way since the days that rape reports regularly included what the victim was wearing (especially if it was "scanty"). Yet victims often question why certain details are used or how they are handled.

■ Be alert to the special impact of photos, graphics and overall presentation. A picture can also cut a thousand times deeper than words. How much blood do readers need to see? What do they learn from yet another photo of a body being loaded into an ambulance?

As Cote and Bucqueroux note, there is no better substitute for judging the sensitivity of a story than for editors to imagine they have a direct link to the story.

"Perhaps the best rule of thumb in such cases is for reporters and editors to reread copy on such sensitive cases one last time, through the prism of how they would feel if the victim were their son or daughter, husband or wife. While that perspective should not automatically carry the argument concerning what goes in or out, it deserves to be part of the overall mix," they say.

Excerpts are from a presentation at the Newspapers and Community Building Symposium, National Newspaper Association annual convention, September 25, 1996, at Nashville, Tenn.

Chapter 5

Reporting suspensions
of high school athletes

Wingers send South St. Paul packing

In a sense, Ricky Jones was trying to fill two pairs of skates Tuesday.

Not only was the junior starting in place of the more experienced Mark Johnson, he is one of two goalies trying to replace Ed Olson, who graduated from the Winger net after last season.

Jones proved he's ready for varsity action by helping the Wingers to a 5-2 nonconference win over South St. Paul in the season opener.

...

Johnson, on suspension for a State High School League violation, will be out one more game before he will be eligible to play.

America's obsession with sports is well documented. Nowhere is community pride stronger than in hometown, high school sports. Check out community newspapers, and sports coverage almost always ranks as a high priority.

And for good reason. The stories are about families, friends and neighbors. Action on the field and reaction on the sidelines and in the stands make good photo opportunities.

A season's ups and downs are discussed — from coffee shops to barber shops to break-rooms at work to dinner tables at home. There are few secrets. The headaches of coaches — including successes and failures of teams — often are common knowledge.

The widespread attention to sports is why community newspapers must report the accomplishments and shortcomings of teams and individual athletes. Newspapers should develop guidelines to specifically address athletes missing a contest due to violations of state high school league or school district rules. Those circumstances often affect the outcome of a contest. Fans deserve to know why athletes, in particular those who are integral to a team's success, are missing from a game — whether it's due to injuries, family emergencies or discipline.

Developing the policy

Policies are only as good as the effort put into developing them. Editors and reporters must talk to as many people as possible within and outside their organizations. The most defensible guidelines are those that reflect consistency and fairness.

Decisions are subjective and no different than newsroom discussions of coverage of government bodies. Meetings of a city council, school board or county board usually demand firsthand coverage. Each of these bodies likely has several committees that meet on either a regular or ad hoc basis. Committees typically don't warrant the same attention. Decisions of whether to send reporters to a meeting, to call for information, or to ignore the meeting altogether are based on the importance of items discussed at the meetings.

Similar criteria govern school extracurricular coverage, especially given the limited resources of small-town newspapers. Not all events meet the same threshold. A speech team or a winless gymnastics team may not command the same coverage as a football team that draws hundreds of fans to each game or a softball team seeking its third consecutive state championship.

The same criteria are used when deciding how to report suspensions of participants in sports and other extracurricular activities. Some situations warrant complete explanations. For example:

A baseball team was poised to make a playoff run. The night before a game, the players gathered for a beer party. They were caught, and several starters were among those suspended. The team, depleted of many key players, lost. The story became front-page news.

A golf team, fresh off a subsection team victory, had high hopes for a state tournament appearance. But officials stripped a golfer of his medals because he was chewing tobacco on the course — a high school league violation — and suspended him from further competition. The newspaper reported the disciplinary action as part of the story. The team, minus its leader, lost in the next round.

A basketball team, picked to be one of the top teams in the state in its class, was cruising along. But an unexpected detour occurred. Two starters were scratched from the starting lineup. One was held out due to disciplinary reasons; the other was out of state visiting a college for a potential sports scholarship. The team lost to a clearly inferior opponent, and the newspaper, in a sentence, explained the reasons for each player's absence.

(One reaction to this story was noteworthy: The parents of the boy who was on a recruiting trip were pleased the distinction was made between the reasons for the players' absences.)

Other situations are not so sharply defined. For example:

Suspension of a third-string varsity football player who hadn't been on the field for a single snap. His absence was hardly noticed on a squad of 30-plus players.

Suspension of a reserve basketball player who had seen little playing time. Her absence was clearly noticed on a team of nine players. She watched the game in street clothes in the bleachers one row behind the bench.

Suspension of cheerleaders for violation of high school league rules at a state tournament. The incident happened 60 miles away, but word traveled quickly in certain community circles.

Implementing the policy

In most cases, brevity is the best practice when acknowledging suspensions. In this regard, there is a distinct difference between reporting the mistakes of high school athletes and the missteps of college or professional athletes.

An example is the story that led this chapter. Yes, the story chronicling the hometown victory carried a banner headline on the sports page. But the goalie's suspension was mentioned in the last sentence of a 12-inch story. For some readers, though — especially the players — even that was too much attention. The team carried its protest further than the usual phone call to the sports staff or letter to the editor: The players and coach refused interviews after their next game, played three days later. The newspaper still covered the game with a play-by-play account. Quotes were used from the visiting, and losing, coach.

The third paragraph of the report read:

"The players and Coach Randy Lewis declined comment after the game in a unified protest over a paragraph in Tuesday's paper about a player who was serving a suspension."

The newspaper deemed it important to state why the story carried no comments from the home team. The reporter was equally careful not to restate the suspended player's name.

The coach and players, having made their point, returned to granting interviews after the next game. The rest of the season proceeded without incident.

In reporting suspensions, one method is to make a distinction between violations of state high school league rules and school district rules without going into details. High school leagues oversee drinking and drug violations, and school districts govern academic eligibility, so those aware of the differences will have a clue as to the violations.

Reporting suspensions of high school athletes

In most cases, suspensions warrant one report only with a mention of how many games an athlete will miss. Exceptions will surface, and policies must allow flexibility. If a suspended athlete returns to action and plays a key role in a critical game, it's difficult not to refer to his or her previous absence.

One legal — and significant — roadblock cannot be overlooked when reporting suspensions: The identity of students may well be classified as private data under state law. School officials might even be subject to civil penalties if they release information. Newsrooms often can still get the information because it is so widespread in small towns. Coaches and school officials may go "off the record," or parents or players may confirm suspensions.

Newspapers must be cautioned on two fronts, however. First, reporters must be sure their information is correct. Second, reporters must be committed to tracking down violations, even if information about them is not readily available. Coaches and parents will complain loudly if all violations aren't treated the same.

Reporters also shouldn't forget — or be afraid — to talk to coaches and players about an incident. Those involved may be willing to talk about the lessons learned. Few newspapers pursue that story because it probably is uncomfortable to do so. But it arguably is the most powerful and constructive angle in discussing sports suspensions — and would command high readership.

Explaining the policy

The immense popularity of school activities means readers will scrutinize a policy of reporting student suspensions.

In the minds of most coaches and readers, small-town newspapers are supposed to be civic boosters, especially when it comes to student athletes. Reporting suspensions inevitably will draw complaints that newspapers are sensationalizing and capitalizing on "bad" news. Editors also should expect the charge that such reporting will have long-lasting, negative effects on kids. In the minds of critics, the reports have no place in newspapers. The people who need to know about disciplinary action have been informed or will find out, they say.

Those arguments should be rejected outright. An effective way to refute such falsehoods is to collect a year's worth of clippings — game reports, feature stories, photos, columns, box scores, stories from school board meetings — that touch on youth sports. Then separate the items into two piles — one of positive, or at least neutral, coverage, and another of negative coverage.

The number of positive stories will dwarf the negative reports. Even among the negative stories — unless there are extraordinary circumstances — reports of disciplinary action will likely represent just a few sentences tucked within a larger story.

Suspensions, to be sure, are embarrassing and maybe even hurtful to the affected individuals, families, friends and teammates. But suspensions also are news, especially when they have an impact on a team. A suspension is one of the facts of a game report.

Sports staffs are bound to miss some suspensions if they cover multiple teams in several communities. That does not mean newspapers should ignore obvious news — and the truth — especially when fans are asking why key players are absent. Public interest is especially intense when suspensions occur on championship-caliber teams.

Editors must ask themselves whether community newspapers can accurately and in good conscience report on athletic events without referring to missing players — especially when the circumstances and consequences are so public.

A Minneapolis high school basketball team — and two players — drew statewide attention in Minnesota metropolitan newspapers when the team culminated its 30-0 season with a state championship — even as two players sat on the bench due to poor school grades and attendance. The lesson was instructive, especially in a society where the preoccupation with sports — and the emphasis on winning — has come at the expense of other values.

The final step in developing and implementing policies is communicating it to readers. Following is Editor Jim Pumarlo's column in the *Red Wing Republican Eagle*:

Why we print sports suspensions

Is the suspension of high school athletes news? The R-E thinks so, particularly when it affects a game's outcome. We routinely identify those suspended; it's a longstanding policy.

By identifying a youth, are we really looking out for his or her best welfare? We think so, though it may not be immediately recognized by the youth, parents or coach.

The issue goes beyond sports. It quite often involves chemical health and as such is part of a far greater community issue.

Not all agree with the publication of names, and we've heard about it, especially with the rash of suspensions the past few weeks. We do not take the issue lightly, and have spent several hours in meetings and seeking the opinions of others. They represent parents, coaches, fans, athletic boosters, social workers, chemical dependency workers and school boards. Our employees have had personal experiences, and we've looked into the policies of other newspapers.

Tuesday morning I spent an hour with about 12 coaches and school administrators. Coaches generally seem opposed to our policy, though not without exception. It's important for coaches — and readers — to understand our policy.

Players are suspended for a variety of reasons — from academic and disciplinary to alcohol and tobacco violations. A suspension may be for a game, a couple of weeks or even longer.

Missing players can affect a team's performance. That's the primary reason we report them. It's part of the game story. If a player is injured, it's reported. If someone is out for other reasons, that ought to be told, too.

There are other reasons for telling the truth:

■ Suspended players, looking perfectly healthy, sit on the bench during a game. Fans deserve to be told why.

■ Players may miss a game for other legitimate reasons. A general statement — "several players were missing either due to suspensions or injuries" — unfairly brands them all.

■ In most cases — particularly those involving tobacco or alcohol violations — players have a choice whether to be involved in an activity which may result in suspension. Before they can play athletics, they sign a contract to abide by rules of the Minnesota State High School League. Players get suspended for actual consumption of alcohol or tobacco. Previously, youths were guilty simply by association.

■ The overwhelming volume of news about players is "good news." It may involve the winning score, the decisive volley, the perfect dive, etc. It seems to us that we send the wrong message to young people if we report only the feats that make them heroes and not the mistakes that reveal them as human.

Moreover, we think a case can be made for constructing suspensions as "good news." Each report is an acknowledgement that coaches are holding youths accountable for their actions. It's a positive reflection on playing by the rules as opposed to winning at any cost.

Is the R-E sensationalizing suspensions only to sell more newspapers? We're insulted by such criticism. If that was our intent, we'd run a photo and put the name in page-one headlines. Rather, our style is to make the report as courteous as possible and generally in a simple sentence.

We do have general guidelines which are constantly reviewed. Our thinking has been changed during the past few weeks.

Names are printed for varsity players only, unless there are extenuating circumstances. For example, if four players are suspended — one dresses for varsity and the others don't — fairness dictates that they be treated alike.

Suspensions henceforth will be acknowledged by the word "suspension" only. Generally, no further details as to the type of suspension are necessary.

If possible, suspensions are noted when they occur, and then in a simple statement of fact. Typically, that's the last mention we'll make.

Critics charge double standards in reporting these violations of high school policy. What about the youth who gets picked up for illegal alcohol consumption, but remains nameless? What about the one who is withheld from band or speech competition for rules violations?

By society's own standards, sports are a class apart. Community interest has dictated that the R-E cover high school sports on a day-to-day basis, unlike other extracurricular activities.

One high school booster reminded me of the credo of a longtime Winger basketball coach. He preached to his players that they were held to higher standards, and deservedly so. People supported the programs with tax dollars. People paid to watch them play.

We view the issue of suspensions — particularly those involving alcohol and tobacco — in the larger context of a communitywide concern. We've observed and often endorsed the community's efforts toward education and prevention. We've seen the school district, the city, the county and the United Way commit dollars and resources to fighting this problem. We've seen coaches spearhead groups to help athletes deal with everpresent pressures.

We think coaches can use the suspension to work positively with youths, and make them better for it.

It's our intent to make the R-E part of the solution. That's why we've sought advice from all quarters on the issue and will continue to do so.

Meanwhile, our commitment remains to report high school sports in a positive vein. Of all the millions of words written during the course of a high school year, the notation of "suspensions" is minuscule.

Lastly, we quote one of Red Wing's most faithful boosters who we polled on the issue. He acknowledged the increasing number of suspensions, but hadn't really given much thought to it. Pressed a little further, he said it might be a bit embarrassing to the youth. But, he added, "It's the truth."

Chapter 6

Publishing photos
of fatal accident scenes

A city dump truck collided with a motorcyclist, killing the cyclist. A clearly distraught truck driver sat at the scene, consoled by a passer-by. The *Red Wing Republican Eagle*'s photographer, Bill Pond, happened to pass the scene, capturing the full emotions in a photo.

It's a classic example where a picture indeed is worth a thousand words.

The publication of photos of fatal accident scenes can generate intense reaction, especially if spread across the front page. Editors must remember that what's published in the newspaper will become part of a family's permanent record and may represent the final seconds of a person's life.

Developing the policy

Many newspapers have a blanket policy to not publish any photos of fatal accidents in deference to family and friends. Responsible coverage and respect for families of victims should be priorities.

But, as with all sensitive and challenging stories, newspapers cannot forget that fatal accidents are real-life situations. They are news, and word of tragedies spreads quickly.

Publishing accident photos almost always prompts complaints of insensitivity. Editors, especially at community newspapers, should feel

Photo by Bill Pond. Used with permission of the Red Wing Republican Eagle.

comfortable in rejecting that charge. Often, readers lump community newspapers with big-city media. Many small-town editors themselves cringe while watching television reporters flock to accident scenes and push microphones and cameras into the faces of anyone available. They know they can do better.

Here are a couple of parameters for evaluating photos from accident scenes:

■ Don't show body parts. Nothing will incense readers more than photos showing the anatomy of victims. The gravity and enormity of an accident can be easily conveyed through other photos from the scene.

■ Avoid showing blood. Photos usually can be easily cropped to eliminate distasteful sections.

Does this mean newspapers should reject all photos that show evidence of a body? What if a sheet is draped over a body?

That's a difficult call, and newspapers probably approach it in different ways. Decisions must be guided by individual circumstances. For example, newspapers should think twice if a body sheet is the focal point of a photo. However, if a covered body is at the edge of a scene — and the rest of the photo is compelling — editors might find the photo acceptable. It's important to remember that readers who strongly object to such photos will complain, regardless of what is published.

As always, editors should look beyond the newsroom in developing policies. Include employees from other departments, and then talk with appropriate individuals within the community.

Victims are people, too

Reporters also should remember the lives of the victims. The biggest complaint from many families is that their final, lasting image of a loved one is a photo of a tangled gnarl of cars. The report may have great detail of the tragic circumstances but just a few sentences about the victims.

Friends often are eager to share comments about the deceased. Contacting families is often an uncomfortable task, but newspapers should not rule it out. Reporters might be surprised at how forthcoming parents, siblings or grandparents are. But there are proper avenues to approach family members — tips that should be included in any policy for reporting on these circumstances.

Small-town newspapers already may have connections with a family. A friend of a friend can make an initial contact.

Even in close-knit communities, however, newspapers may find it difficult to reach a family. The people may be newcomers. They may live in town but work elsewhere. Or they may simply keep to themselves. There still are ways to contact families without being intrusive.

Staff at funeral homes can be excellent liaisons. They know who is acting as a family contact. It may be an aunt or uncle, a cousin or a special friend.

Other individuals make good connections, too. Talk to neighbors and co-workers who are close to the family. A review of the obituary might provide leads, too. Did the deceased belong to any organizations? Did they win any special awards? Were they in the military? People may be hesitant to talk, but just doing the research and making contacts can lead to a solid story.

Just as there are right ways to approach families of victims, there are wrong ways, too.

In one devastating accident a family lost a child and had another put into intensive care. Imagine the surprise — and disgust — when the family received a telephone call in the intensive care unit from a reporter at a metropolitan newspaper. The reporter had made his way through the operators by posing as a family member. The reporter's insensitivity and lack of professionalism certainly made that family wary of future contact with any news organization.

One important step is for editors to meet with law enforcement agencies and other emergency response personnel who are routinely at accident scenes. It's important for both sides to understand and appreciate each other's rights and responsibilities. Reporters and photographers may approach an accident, stating their right to get the news. The responsibility of officers is to secure a scene and protect the individuals involved. The two purposes often can collide. It's beneficial for all parties to sit down and draw up ground rules in a calm atmosphere, rather than confront each other under the stress of an accident scene.

Implementing the policy

Publishing photos of accidents can have a positive effect. The accident highlighted in this chapter occurred at a particularly deadly stretch of highway. Improvements were under consideration for several crossings, including this one. The photo put a spotlight on the situation.

Accidents provide opportunity for follow-up reports, too. Newspapers can document the history of accidents at particular sites, and conduct a statistical review of accidents citywide. The report can note where accidents resulted in serious injuries and/or fatalities. At a minimum, the report will educate motorists.

Explaining the policy

Reporting fatal accidents in small communities can have a large impact. Word spreads quickly and many people will know the people involved.

In the case that led this chapter, the image of the accident — the motorcycle pinned beneath the truck tire — was most unsettling for the family. The family asked that the newspaper publish a photo of the memorial erected at the scene. The request was reasonable, and the photo accompanied the editor's column, which explained the decision to publish the photos.

Some stories about fatal accidents prompt different questions.

For example, should a story state that unopened beer cans were found at an accident scene if authorities have not yet released the blood-alcohol content of the drivers? Should a story state whether everyone was wearing seat belts? Should a story state whether motorcyclists were wearing helmets?

Reporting these facts can be painful to family members and friends. But the information also can be integral to a story. These facts, and others, are part of official police reports. They help readers understand why an accident occurred. They can offer lessons to others.

The final step in developing and implementing policies is communicating with readers. Following is Editor Jim Pumarlo's column in the *Red Wing Republican Eagle*:

The photos said it all

A city dump truck and a motorcycle collided at noon last Thursday just a few miles out of downtown, killing the cyclist and leaving the city worker in shock. Officials at City Hall issued a statement offering condolences to the family of the victim and took steps to help employees deal with the emotional stress.

The R-E carried the story the next day, complete with photos of the despondent driver being consoled by a passer-by and of the accident scene. The photos indeed were worth the proverbial thousand words.

One reader, whose comments were not published, called to say she could not find a single person who thought we should have run the photos, especially of the truck driver. A fourth-grader even threw down the newspaper in disgust, she said.

Reporting tragedies — in words and photos — is always a challenge. But the fact remains: Fatal accidents are significant events in the life of a community. No information travels faster than that of a tragic accident.

In this case, especially, the photos captured the essence of the moment. No words were necessary to describe the emotion of the truck driver, Steve Jones.

"I thought the photo was accurate," said Jones by telephone earlier this week, obviously still trying to deal with the death of the motorcyclist, Rick Johnson. "The photo had to be accurate. It was a life scene situation."

We had called Jones to ask how he felt about the R-E's coverage. Our call was not to seek endorsement of the photo, but to explain that it's part of the difficult job of printing the news.

We considered the feelings of the Johnson family as well when we chose to run a photo of the motorcycle and truck. We respect those who disagree with our decision. A letter elsewhere on this page from Jill Hanson, Rick's sister, expresses her dismay with our coverage.

Criticism from readers was no surprise. It even was expected as we selected the photos, knowing they will be part of the permanent record of the tragedy.

The decision to print the photos was not a snap judgment, and we do have guidelines.

We refrain as best we can from publishing photographs that show the deceased. The more effective photos often are those of bystanders and friends at the scene. The rest of the information can be conveyed in the story.

Some readers always will contend that such coverage is sensationalism. We readily accept opposing viewpoints — and criticism when it's warranted — but we reject the blanket charge.

The R-E, in contrast with the television industry, is quite sensitive regarding graphic photos and descriptive text. Often those involved in bad accidents are neighbors and acquaintances of people at the newspaper. This accident was no different.

But our responsibility is to report the news — good and bad. Violence and grief are very much a part of everyday life. In this case, we deemed it appropriate to show the tragic moment, but we do not minimize the fact that there are strong differences of opinion.

Not all readers accept newsroom policies on the reporting of sensitive issues. Newspapers will be stronger for accepting — and publishing — criticism, and then using it to review policies.

Following are two letters to the editor that appeared in the *Red Wing Republican Eagle* in response to the publication of photos of the fatal accident. Names of the writers and individuals involved in the accident have been changed.

Family member shocked by accident photos

To the editor:

I pray that the Lord will guide me as I write these words.

The tragedy of the loss of our beloved Rick Johnson has been beyond description. Our pain has been overwhelming, and only our faith and the outpouring of love and support make it even slightly bearable.

I know I speak for my entire family when I say these words. Now I will speak for myself.

The coverage by the *Republican Eagle* was a shock and a bitter disappointment. Color photographs of the accident scene made the motorcycle on which Rick was killed visible. Although any anger I felt at the truck driver dissipated when I saw his body slumped and grief-stricken, this forgiveness would have come anyway. The speeding of that process was not worth the added shame and agony to him and his family by blasting his name and image across the front page.

The complete circumstances of the accident are unknown to me at this time, but it seems ironic the newspaper had so much information and could relay that "Johnson hit the single-axle dump truck broadside." From what I understand, this was simply a terrible accident and there was nothing my brother could have done to avoid it.

Rick was an incredibly skilled and careful driver, and was wearing nearly 50 pounds of protective gear to drive less than two miles to his workplace. Some comfort comes from knowing he died doing something he loves.

I ask that the R-E have compassion for Rick's family and friends in the weeks ahead as more information about the accident becomes available. Never again should a person have to experience the compounding of loss I felt when I saw that cover story. When my youngest brother went to the newspaper office to obtain extra copies of the obituary, he was asked to pay half-price.

While I realize that knowledge of circumstances in a situation such as this aids us in acceptance and understanding, there is a difference between that and morbid curiosity. Let us keep in mind that we are all members of the human family, and take a stand to let the media know we no longer will tolerate such insensitivity.

Anyone who knew Rick loved him. He was truly a unique and beautiful creation, and he saw worth and goodness in everyone. His sense of humor, kindness, intelligence and ambition are but a fraction of the things that I remember about him. His nephews and niece adored him, and he them. I look forward to the day when I will see Rick again, as the Lord has promised.

Jill Hanson

Editor excels at explaining news decisions

To the editor:

I have been impressed for some time with the thoroughness and thoughtfulness of Editor Jim Pumarlo's responses to readers in his editor's column.

The responses are always very well thought out and explained to readers in a logical way. The decisions are drawn from looking at many perspectives, public sensitivity, the public's right to know, newspaper ethics, and accuracy in reporting community issues.

I am impressed with the overview he takes of public issues, and I am particularly impressed with his ability to express that overview in a way that is logical and concise.

Many people seem to look at issues from only one perspective, which is probably why they get so upset when that "only one perspective" is not shared. Life is not that simple. There are many ways to look at any issue, and I have great respect for the way the editor integrates and balances those perspectives in editorial decisions.

Explaining decisions or beliefs as he does allows people to at least understand that decisions are — or should be — made after a reflective and well thought-out process. He describes that process well. I commend the citizens of Red Wing for their fine editor.

Janet Ryan

Chapter 7
Covering business

"You won't read that in the newspaper," the person says. "After all, it's about one of the paper's biggest advertisers."

Nothing draws the attention of publishers more quickly than customers who threaten to take their business elsewhere if something gets into print. Stakes are especially high if customers are major advertisers or prominent individuals.

Advertiser ultimatums and the resulting predicaments cannot be ignored, especially at small-town newspapers. Editors are right to weigh requests. But news decisions should be made within the context of underlying policies, and guidelines should be in writing. Owners and publishers must think of repercussions to the credibility of their products if news decisions are altered on the basis of *who* instead of *what* is the subject. Circumstances can prove especially challenging if customers have personal relationships with owners and publishers.

Newspapers have broad justification in printing certain stories that customers might pressure to have withheld. Confrontations between newsrooms and advertisers often are rooted in a poor understanding between the message and the messenger. Take, for example, a city council that suspended a store's tobacco license for selling cigarettes to minors. The council was imposing the punishment; the newspaper was simply reporting the penalty.

Business news — good and bad

Nearly 50 employees would be out of jobs after an insurance company, with headquarters in another state, announced the closing of its local office. The newspaper learned of the decision from one of the workers and carried a report two days after the announcement. The parent company, when contacted by a reporter, grudgingly released information but never issued a press release.

In contrast, the same parent company met with local news staff when it originally purchased the hometown business. Management made it a point to speak with the newspaper the day of the announcement.

Everyone is eager to share what's considered good news, but reluctant to talk about bad news. The same thing happens, naturally, with public officials. But there's a major difference: State laws often guarantee the press access to government news — good and bad. The press does not have the same level of access to information on private business.

Restricted access, however, does not make such events any less newsworthy. Indeed, it's arguable that news about employers has even greater meaning in smaller communities than some decisions coming from City Hall. After all, it's news about friends and neighbors.

Business start-ups, acquisitions and expansions, promotions and labor strikes are news. Some events will reflect positively on businesses; others will not. It remains in the best interests of companies to be forthcoming on both counts. Businesses willing to share bad news will find newspapers much more willing to listen when they pitch good news, too.

Newspapers also can benefit by sharing the responsibility of communication. Editors will have better luck prying bad news from a company if they have cultivated solid coverage of local business. That is, don't expect cooperation from business owners if the only time they are contacted is when a story might reflect poorly on their company.

Labor strikes, contracts

Work stoppages, especially at major employers, can be terribly divisive and disruptive to communities. Negotiation of new contracts can be equally noteworthy. Both pose challenges for coverage.

Pickets make strikes visible events, but that does not guarantee easy access to information. Union representatives and striking workers have a propensity to volley charges and talk openly against management. In contrast, management often is reluctant to say much of anything, and often is constrained by labor laws. Reporters must flush out the facts, identifying those points where the two sides agree and disagree.

Communities also can be on watch when major employers negotiate new contracts, even without a threat of work stoppage. Resolution of new contracts is newsworthy. Specifics of the settlement can be a barometer for other looming wage negotiations.

No laws require that private companies release salary information, and many businesses keep details private for competitive reasons. Newspapers can compromise by presenting an overview of contracts including such standard information as percentage increase in wages. It usually is to employers' advantage to release something. Rumors often fly about what's transpiring at the bargaining table, even when talks are progressing relatively smoothly. Stating the facts can put issues to rest.

News versus advertising

A restaurant gets new owners. That's news. The same restaurant issues a press release about the popularity of its special home-made soup. That's an ad.

An investment firm relocates. That's news. The company announces a new line of annuities. That's an ad.

A retailer opens in town. That's news. The same merchant sends press releases about grand openings and successive anniversary sales. Those are ads.

Such events occur routinely and underscore the misunderstanding among many business owners about what's legitimately a news story and what's strictly a promotion that should be advertised.

Business news should be just that — news. Reports should include announcements of new businesses, key changes such as a new location, new management or major remodeling, or significant developments in operations.

But newspapers should not, despite pressure from advertisers, routinely report on changes that relate directly to marketing strategies. A new department, added product lines, informal staff reorganization, expanded services or reoccurring sales promotions with customer giveaways all properly fall under advertising.

Ad representatives routinely forward requests for news coverage from clients. Some items pass the litmus test, and others do not. It's important for ad staffs to understand the news rationale. Once newspapers ignore the barrier between news and advertising — and accept advertisers' releases carte blanche — they better be prepared. Advertisers watch their competitors closely, and soon releases will roll into the office. More customers — rather than paying to market their products and services — will try to replace, or at least augment, their ad budgets with a regular dose of releases. That means less money for newspapers and ad staffs.

Editors and advertising managers can usually identify customers who routinely submit releases under the guise of legitimate news. The best approach is to tell the clients directly: If editors accept one release that crosses the boundary, they will have a difficult time saying no to the next business. Soon it will boil down to a battle of public relations machines.

Conflicts between news and advertising always will flare. Resolving differences will be easier if newspapers develop policies endorsed by both news and advertising departments.

Letters to the editor

Community newspapers are supposed to be boosters of local business, right? So why shouldn't they publish letters complimentary of stores that represent the best in customer service, or offer top-notch quality merchandise, or deliver the best bargains?

Are newspapers also prepared to print letters that complain about restaurants that serve cold food, or stores that don't honor policies for returned merchandise, or businesses that have unsightly junk piles on their grounds?

In short, newspapers are wise to adopt policies that reject most comments — whether complaints or compliments — if they refer to private business. The exception is if letters address public issues.

It's fair comment for readers to question the wisdom of closing a road to assist a grocery store expansion. Out of bounds, however, are remarks that oppose a tax subsidy for the same expansion because the store's new format will force customers to bag their own groceries.

Being a referee for these decisions can be tricky. Consider a big-box retailer seeking to locate in smaller communities, an increasingly common scenario. Discussing the merits of the proposal inevitably results in a debate about existing stores — their merchandise, their prices and their service. To squelch all comments would be wrong. But editors must be careful that the public exchange focuses on broad issues and does not denigrate existing or prospective merchants.

The letters policy cuts both ways. Newspapers that reject publication of negative comments about private business should not accept positive comments.

The policy may appear that it favors negative over positive comments. For example, a newspaper publishes a letter critical of a store's display on a public sidewalk. It rejects a letter complimentary of a store's window display. Once again, the decision rests on whether an issue is in the public or private arena.

Exceptions always surface. Comments should be judged on individual circumstances.

Reports can backfire

How many times have newspapers sought to localize a business story?

What is the impact of higher interest rates on home sales? Are travel agencies feeling the effects of reduced international travel following terrorist attacks? How do banks feel about legislation that would invite new competition?

The best community newspapers distinguish themselves by bringing state and national issues into local perspective. That's an especially effective tool in expanding local business coverage. But it can backfire.

Take an example of new banking regulations. The story broke early afternoon, giving a news staff almost a full cycle to prepare a story outlining local impact for the next edition. A reporter immediately called a handful of banks. Three spokesmen were immediately available. Messages were left at the other two; one called in the morning but the other one was unavailable. The newspaper ran the story to keep it timely, then waited for the predictable call. The president of the unmentioned bank complained. From his perspective, the omission made it appear that the bank didn't exist.

Newspapers always run this hazard, but editors should not stop the practice. Rather, they should write these stories regularly and rotate the companies they contact. It's usually impossible to call every affected business. But if newspapers do such stories frequently, businesses will understand that they'll get their opportunity to be in the newspaper.

Noteworthy individuals: 'Just this one time'

The cause-effect relationship with some advertisers is fairly direct. Print a "negative" story about their business, they say, and they'll withdraw their advertising.

Other conflicts are more subtle but just as challenging for editors. Complainants do not always have to be major advertisers. They might be prominent individuals who threaten to make life miserable for newspapers if certain information is published.

Consider these scenarios.

A politician's son or daughter is suspended from a sports team for drinking. A retail store owner files for bankruptcy. A prominent citizen gets a divorce. These situations and many more can prompt requests to withhold information.

Some information is classified as public data, and usually should be reported by newspapers in their roles as recorders of community history. Newsrooms should deviate from guidelines only when extenuating circumstances dictate. The message must be delivered to all customers — all readers — including the biggest advertisers.

Newspapers often are asked why they can't look the other way — just this one time. Editors, and publishers, should know better. There rarely is such a thing as "just this one time."

The biggest fallacy is that overlooking a sensitive item can be dismissed as a harmless oversight. More often than not, decisions to look the other way will come back to haunt editors, especially in small towns where word circulates. The information eventually surfaces, and newspapers usually end up printing it. The result is tarnished newspaper reputations and embarrassment to the individuals who were trying to suppress it.

Grand openings, anniversaries

Grand openings are news when they occur at the actual opening of a business. They are not news when they are celebrated three months after a store has opened. Stores seeking coverage for after-the-fact ribbon cuttings should be directed to the advertising department.

Rejecting an advertiser's request also is touchy business; news and advertising departments must be aligned on when grand openings warrant coverage. How the events are covered is just as important. The store and its employees are the news; grand openings should not be another photo opportunity for the mayor or chamber of commerce officials.

Newspapers also should develop guidelines for coverage of anniversary celebrations. Benchmarks of 50, 75 or 100 years usually are automatic stories. But editors should be prepared for requests to commemorate five, 10 and 25 years. Or how about struggling merchants who have survived their first year?

Discussions intensify when merchants point out that they also are spending money to advertise their events. Editors must stand firm on policies, but they'll be on much stronger foundation if they exercise responsibility in ongoing business coverage.

Visit with publishers

Editors might have to deliver their most persuasive arguments to publishers. Owners and publishers must understand the importance of consistency and fairness in news coverage. They must participate at the ground level when newsrooms develop news policies, especially for those policies concerning coverage of sensitive and challenging topics.

Not all policies will have unanimous approval within the office, and that is healthy. Differences of opinion will guarantee that policies will be under continual review, which only can strengthen decision-making.

At the same time, those individuals who explain and implement policies must present a united front when interacting with readers. The message must be shared and endorsed by everyone, beginning with top management.

News and advertising departments must operate closely — but independently. If customers purchase an ad, they should expect professional and courteous service and a good return on their investments.

But there should be no link between how much advertisers spend — or how influential particular individuals are in a community — and how much news coverage their corresponding businesses receive.

Just as advertisers are entitled to courteous service by their ad representatives, they should expect and receive from editors a courteous and clear explanation of the separation between news and advertising.

Chapter 8
Everyday decisions

Some small-town newspapers just bypass the difficulties of reporting on tough and sensitive issues by implementing a blanket policy of not reporting them.

That's unfortunate. A "one size fits all" policy is shortsighted.

It's a good bet that most newspapers do not report suicides. Many also shy away from publishing photos of fatal accident scenes. And a good number probably do not report names of suspended high school athletes.

But many other news items require delicate handling. The stories may not be as emotionally charged as a suicide, but they still involve elements that can generate reaction. Many of the items arise every day in small towns.

Newsrooms should discuss approaches and establish guidelines for what gets published. The most important practice may be laying the groundwork for how situations will be handled or explained to customers.

Editorials

A newspaper has little choice but to identify all stores fined for selling cigarettes to underage youths. But the coverage still will draw wrath from certain businesses.

In contrast, a newspaper can be selective in topics it addresses on its editorial page. The positions are not welcomed by all, such as the decision to endorse a proposed commercial development — "The project is envisioned to bolster the community as a regional retail center but also will result in either buy-outs or relocations of several existing businesses." Courageous publishers and editors take those stances, regardless of potential repercussions.

Vigorous editorial pages are the conscience of vibrant communities. Newspapers that fulfill that role — many regard it as a responsibility — should anticipate calls from their detractors, which can include advertisers.

A reader asks how a newspaper can endorse city council candidates who are pro-downtown and ignore interests of other commercial districts. Another asks how a newspaper can support a tax subsidy for a business expansion when it will result in higher taxes for neighboring properties.

Newspaper management must take measured steps in all editorial positions and be cognizant of their impact. That does not mean newspapers should shy away from controversy. Rather, editorials themselves should state the difficulty of an issue but point out that a particular position is being advocated for the overall good.

Complaints of bias miss the point that editorials, by definition, advance a singular point of view. In a way, editorials are similar to courtroom arguments. Opposing attorneys may begin with the same set of facts but are selective in what they use to try to persuade jurors to reach a certain conclusion.

Editorials and columns often are misunderstood by readers. They require a great deal of care and research by writers, especially when the commentary addresses sensitive topics. Nothing can be more delicate than encouraging readers to support certain individuals and to reject others for elected office. All these individuals are friends and neighbors of many people. They may have connections to newspaper employees, including the publisher and editor.

Editorials can be complimentary or critical. They can be controversial, and they might challenge people and individuals.

Editorials are positioned as a reasoned opinion utilizing a set of facts. They are not, however, intended to be the "right" or "sole" opinion on an issue. Indeed, letters to the editor written in response sometimes can be more persuasive than the original editorial.

That point is frequently misinterpreted by those who may be the subject of editorials. It's most painful for individuals — for example, those who may not be endorsed by newspapers for an election. Non-endorsement should not reflect on people's character. Rather, editorials represent newspapers' judgments on which individuals will best represent the interests of communities on elected boards.

In many respects, editorials are held to a higher standard than news articles. From the perspective of newspapers, that underscores several basic "dos" and "don'ts." Among them:

■ Editorials should stick to public issues. Private businesses and individuals typically are off limits unless involved with an issue that enters the public arena.

■ Editorials should not unfairly ridicule or tarnish a person's reputation.

■ Editorials should not distort facts to purposely mislead the public by creating a false impression.

■ Most important, a newspaper's opinion page should be a forum for all opinions. It especially should encourage and welcome opinions contrary to newspapers' stated positions.

Obituaries

Obituaries are staples of small-town newspapers, and they also involve sensitive circumstances. Grieving families face dictates of what can be published in newspapers that still print free obituaries.

Death reports vary from paid notices to news obituaries to news stories. For paid notices, individuals provide and pay for exactly what they want printed. Newspapers still should have guidelines to ensure obituaries are tasteful and do not raise any red flags — such as potential legal action.

News judgment must be exercised in the case of prominent individuals and other residents whose deaths warrant separate stories. Colorful details in a news story are not only acceptable but desirable.

A third category — news obituaries — can fall into two groups. Some papers will choose to write news obituaries about select individuals, either because they were prominent or because they led interesting lives. At other newspapers — where the number of deaths is manageable — staff reporters write news obituaries for everyone.

In both cases, reporters review and report facts from information provided by families. The practice allows subjectivity and freedom to carry more detail on certain aspects of individuals' lives. But newspapers still should have guidelines for news obits.

Many community newspapers continue to publish all obituaries free as a public service, though they are presented in a standard format. Guidelines are required as the number of notices varies and obituaries can be written by a variety of staff writers.

Developing these policies is the first step, and then they must be communicated clearly and regularly. Funeral homes should be supplied copies of what newspapers accept.

Engagements, weddings, 'people' items

Readers expect newspapers to have a place for these and other mainstay "people" items — births, graduations, military service, academic and employment honors.

It's normal practice to publish these announcements, but the challenge is sorting out the accompanying information. Are parents and/or grandparents of the honorees listed? Are former residents recognized? How much biographical information is included? Editors must be prepared to field these and other requests. Names of neighbors are the bread-and-butter of community newspapers. At the same time, newspapers must draw limits.

Wedding write-ups, once accepted as run-of-the-mill news items, now raise questions. Newspapers are placed in the position of defining what constitutes marriage, prompted by the increasing numbers of gay and lesbian couples who participate in ceremonies of civil unions. How newspapers handle the requests for publication — and how they explain their policies — is a sensitive issue for the participants as well as readers.

Proclamations

Proclamations are great promotional tools for many organizations. They're wonderful for club scrapbooks, and that's where they belong. Proclamations in and of themselves are not news.

Requests to publicize proclamations are frequent at community newspapers. Organizations believe a hometown newspaper should report all of their activities — including proclamations.

Still, proclamations should not necessarily be ignored — it comes down to newsworthiness. Are local festivities planned? Will a special event be held? Those might be newsworthy events.

If newspapers routinely cover organizations' newsworthy events, editors should have little problem rejecting routine proclamations.

Police/court reports

Police blotters are important parts of newspapers that help readers keep up with public safety news.

Imagine an item in the police blotter listing a DWI. The initial report would include information from police or court complaints, but little from the individual. The newspaper has an obligation to inform readers, but also must make it clear that the individual has only been charged at this point.

The first opportunity for the defendant to present his or her side of a case will be during a court appearance. Reporters should recognize this and give the defense arguments proper attention. In other words, don't put the prosecutor's arguments on page one and bury the defense's rebuttal on the jump page.

In similar vein, give equal treatment to initial and follow-up stories, especially if charges prove unfounded. If the first story is on Page 1, the follow-up likely should be there, too.

Blind-sided attacks

How many times has someone appeared before a city council, county board or school board to unleash criticism about an individual or organization? Reporters have little difficulty presenting a balanced report — getting both sides of the story — if the accused is at the meeting.

But what if the individual is not present? And what if deadlines require stories to be written that night?

Stories have more meaning if the accused have a chance to respond — even if they offer no comment. Reporters should do what's necessary to present a balanced story. That might require leaving a meeting early or enlisting the help of another reporter.

Public employees

Public employees are under the microscope for good reason. They are paid by taxpayer dollars, and they decide how to spend taxpayer dollars. They should expect that their salaries will be published and their decisions scrutinized.

Editors must remember, however, that even public officials have private lives that should be respected. The line is not always clear. Do newspapers publish a reader's inquiry regarding the poor condition of rental property owned by the mayor? Probably. But would newspapers write about a municipal sanitation worker who declares personal bankruptcy? Probably not.

Newspapers should be assertive, and responsible, in reporting on public employees.

Diversity

Long gone are the days when diverse populations were limited to urban areas. Sizable minority populations are common in many communities, yet many newspapers still treat diversity and its accompanying issues as a relatively new phenomenon.

Devoting one or two staff meetings to the challenge and offering token coverage will be seen as just that by readers. The only way newspapers will improve coverage of the changing character of their communities is by consciously addressing the subject in everyday newsroom discussions and decisions.

Diversity is not limited to racial backgrounds. It includes other things such as socioeconomic levels, religions and sexual orientations. They all add to the richness of everyday life, which newspapers should reflect in their coverage.

Elections

Election coverage is a demanding task. Every aspect is scrutinized by readers, especially if they believe newspapers have a political bias. It matters little that a bias is limited to the opinion page; most readers do not make a distinction between editorials and news stories.

The enormity of the task demands that staffs thoroughly think through all aspects of coverage and establish policies.
- What are the guidelines for letters to the editor?
- What are criteria for candidate endorsements?

■ How are initial candidate announcements handled, and what are the benchmarks for continuing coverage?
■ When are photos used?
■ When does a story warrant front-page placement?
■ How are 11th-hour charges — or any accusation for that matter — reported?

Candidates and their supporters will keep close watch on how newspapers handle these and other circumstances. The more organized newsrooms are, the better prepared they'll be to handle reader criticism.

Prominent citizens and their families

A state lawmaker refers to strong family values as part of his campaign, then gets a divorce. A top county administrator is cited for drunken driving. Both stories deserve to be written, though editors might disagree on the amount of detail to include.

What if you learn that police crashed a party at the home of a state legislator and youths were caught drinking? No adults were home, and parents probably were unaware of the party. One newspaper faced with this situation reported the home address and identified those youths of legal age, but made no reference to the parent.

Editors often are faced with deciding when to acknowledge a connection between individuals and their families, employers or certain organizations. There is no universal right or wrong in these situations, but they demand consistent consideration. Newsrooms should develop general guidelines, keeping in mind that all circumstances should be reviewed on their individual merits.

Newspapers typically confront these decisions in connection with "bad" news.

Editors should not forget, however, the instances of proud parents and grandparents. Prominent residents, or those residents who expect favorable treatment in their local newspapers, may ask that certain items get published that otherwise would not. Bending the rules for "good" news can produce just as many headaches for editors as looking the other way when "bad" news occurs.

Too much information?

The detrimental health effects of methamphetamine are well documented, and the labs pose significant fire hazards. So why would newspapers publish the ingredients necessary to manufacture the illegal drug? The scope of the methamphetamine problem has prompted law enforcement agencies to assist stores in educating employees to watch for customers who buy large quantities of ingredients needed to manufacture the drug. Perhaps a newspaper's report about meth production could do the same thing.

Newspapers must assess the risk of providing too much information versus the responsibility to educate parents and others about the warning signs of problems such as illegal drug manufacturing. Editors should anticipate when such stories might provoke criticism from readers, and publish an accompanying explanatory note.

Public records

The most defensible policy on public records is to publish all or nothing. Editors should not be placed in the position of judge and jury, determining when someone has a valid request for withholding information.

Editors should expect to regularly field requests about keeping names out of reports of marriages and divorces, bankruptcies, traffic citations, court reports, building permits and many other public records.

Some people never will be convinced about the value of printing public records. Newspapers can stem some criticism if they are prompt with reports. It can be days or even weeks before information is available from the appropriate authorities. News staffs should make regular rounds of the various offices and publish records in a timely manner. Nothing is more embarrassing than publishing a couple's application for a marriage license two months after the wedding.

Workplace accidents

A teacher lost part of a finger during a lab experiment. A worker on an assembly line lost all of his fingers when they were caught in equipment, and eventually won a significant settlement in a civil lawsuit.

Both were sensitive events, and both were news. It's also in the best interests of those involved — employers and employees — to provide accurate information and set the record straight. The teacher's accident is an excellent example. Students throughout the building came home that afternoon and told parents that the teacher had lost an entire hand.

Sketchy details of workplace accidents may be available through police reports or other avenues. That's a first stop for information, but reporters also should try to talk to those involved — even if the story is only a few paragraphs. Some individuals may decline comment, but the attempt should be made.

Outside media attention

Newspapers must be consistent in coverage of sensitive events, no matter the distractions. Attention from outside media can be one of the biggest diversions and tests for small-town news staffs. It's awfully tempting for editors to second-guess themselves and alter coverage to follow the lead of big-city media.

Out-of-town media often swoop into communities for a day or two, and then leave — maybe never setting foot in the town again. Community press shines best by providing steady and consistent coverage of an event from beginning to end.

Chapter 9
Gathering the tough news

Developing policies for tackling tough and sensitive issues is no easy task. It requires thorough and conscientious consultation with people within and outside newspaper offices.

Once guidelines are drawn, however, the hardest work still may lie ahead. Getting facts to report sensitive stories often is challenging, even if information is deemed public under state and federal laws.

One of the biggest misconceptions is that simply because data or meetings are classified as public, authorities will readily answer questions and automatically turn over information. Many editors can attest to the immense time required to educate public officials on data they are required to release. Even when reporters are armed with laws, attorneys and government agencies are likely to balk and take exception.

It's unfortunate, but many small-town news staffs have neither the expertise, nor time and ability to become educated, on the laws in order to challenge government bodies. As a result, important facts and even entire stories go unreported. Newspapers and communities are both losers. Newspapers get accused of covering up a story, and residents are left uninformed.

Editors do not have to become legal experts. There are a variety of avenues to get a story if "official sources" present roadblocks. Following are suggestions for getting information that's often integral to reporting sensitive stories:

■ Ask the question. Reporters often grumble about public officials who are not forthcoming with bad news. But how many reporters have failed to simply ask the question? Officials routinely will remain mum on news that's not particularly flattering to their organizations unless pressed by someone. Asking the question is so obvious that it's often overlooked by reporters.

■ Ask officials to cite the law. Officials may refuse to release information because "they don't have to" or because "they are unsure" of what state law dictates. Neither response passes muster.

Reporters should press officials to cite the law that classifies data as private. In most cases, officials are unable to cite the statute and are withholding information based on a hunch or personal preference.

A basic premise of open-records laws is that all data are classified public and all meetings are deemed open — unless laws specifically say otherwise. If officials can't identify a law, they have no legal justification to withhold information or close a meeting.

As always, the best offense is to be prepared. Reporters usually can anticipate when they'll be challenged. Newsrooms should take the initiative to research laws. Educating officials doesn't mean immediate success; City Hall still might try to stonewall. But reporters will be in far better position to stand their ground if they know the law and have a copy of it in hand.

■ Present a case based on the spirit of the law as well as the letter of the law. Reporters have the best chance of flushing out information from public officials when they can cite the chapter and verse of the law. An even more compelling argument is to press for information based on the spirit of the law — specifically, in the spirit of open government.

Landfill siting may be controversial, but constituents will be more accepting of the process if a county board identifies potential locations from the start. The departure of a controversial department head may not be official until formally accepted, but a city council will do itself a favor by announcing a resignation as soon as it is submitted. The closing of an elementary school may not be on a school board's official agenda for a few weeks, but administration will win higher marks if it informs residents of its intentions when first put on the table.

Public officials should understand the implications of their messages when they respond to the press "no comment," only to verify the information days or weeks later.

■ Do the same with non-governmental entities. Pressing private organizations and businesses for information under the sprit of openness can be more difficult. Open-records laws do not apply to them. Editors and reporters should advance the same arguments nonetheless.

A manufacturer reduced staff by 50 employees. A health-care center settled a nursing contract after protracted negotiations. A chamber of commerce dismissed its director.

All of these events occurred in the private sector, and they were newsworthy. In many communities, these types of developments may be bigger news than local elections. More often than not, this kind of news travels quickly by word of mouth in coffee shops and workplaces and on the street — and the information is not always accurate. Private institutions have a compelling reason to set the record straight before rumors start swirling.

Good news or bad news, routine news or sensitive news — it's in the best interests of the source to deliver the information first.

■ Develop informal networks. All communities have hot spots of conversation. One small-town publisher refers to the five Bs — bars, beauticians, barbers, butchers and bakeries. Editors and reporters should make just as much effort to drop in regularly at these places as they do at the city hall, cop shop or courthouse.

Regular morning roundtables at a coffee shop are excellent venues for picking up on sensitive stories as well as feature stories about local residents. Drop in regularly, and editors will find they'll develop an informal group of correspondents. Some individuals will be waiting to pass along story ideas, especially if they wind up in print on occasion.

■ Lay the groundwork. Newsrooms are quick to demand information when a crisis hits. But how many reporters make regular contacts with news sources? Editors and reporters must develop relationships with public officials if they expect cooperation on getting bad news as well as good news.

Benefits will be mutual. Sources will be more comfortable in pitching stories to newspapers, and reporters will have a better chance of getting answers to tough questions. Give adequate notice.

Another step in laying the groundwork is preparing policies to deal with complicated stories. Deadlines often prevent newsrooms from having time to sort through complicated processes, so it's important to have a policy in place beforehand.

One of the routine challenges facing news staffs is explaining government budgets. How the numbers are presented is critical. Readers will get their impressions about city operations and finances based on the first report. Get the information wrong, and city hall and the newspaper both will suffer.

Yet, consider how the process normally works. Budget preparation can involve weeks, if not months, of work — multiple drafts and countless meetings with staff and workshops with council members. The final product can exceed a hundred pages.

The budget often is given to reporters just days in advance or maybe even the night of the meeting. If a newspaper has waited until then to initiate budget coverage, the result will be disastrous.

Editors should anticipate when a story demands extra homework on the part of reporters and initiate a meeting with city officials.

In the same way, editors should lay the groundwork for other challenging issues whenever possible. If newsrooms are aware that a sensitive court case is scheduled for a hearing, for example, staff should immediately talk about coverage.

It's important to talk to as many people as possible. In court proceedings, for example, a good practice is for reporters to contact prosecuting and defense attorneys and other judicial representatives. Doing advance work will not necessarily get everyone to agree on how particular information should be handled, but individuals will be less surprised by what is published. And there's a good chance the effort will lead to a more balanced — and thus stronger — story.

■ Use confidential sources if necessary, but only as a last resort. Overuse of confidential sources, especially by the Washington, D.C. press corps, has turned many Americans sour on the press. Reporters should avoid attributing information to confidential sources for obvious reason: Grant one request, and precedent is set.

Still, confidential sources sometimes cannot be avoided. Their use, however, demands accuracy. A good rule of thumb is to have confidential information confirmed by at least one, and preferably two, other sources.

Confidential sources often are necessary to flush out sensitive stories that are stonewalled through traditional avenues. Newspapers might get a story eventually, but it will be on the terms of the sources — and often days, or even weeks, after word has circulated. Readers deserve to know news as it happens, and not be held hostage by sources who want to release information at their convenience.

■ Use others in the industry as a resource.

Editors and reporters should look to each other when they run into stumbling blocks. State newspaper associations and other industry groups are a good starting point. Many offer legal "hot line" services. There also are helpful Web sites. They include:

Reporters Committee for Freedom of the Press (www.rcfp.org)
Newspaper Association of America (www.naa.org)
National Newspaper Association (www.nna.org)
Freedom Forum (www.freedomforum.org)
Editor & Publisher (www.editorandpublisher.com)
Society of Professional Journalists (www.spj.org)

Public officials often feel they can simply say "no" to a request, and reporters will go away. It's unfortunate, but many small-town editors do just that because they are busy preparing the next edition. An official "no" should not be the end of an inquiry. Editors will be pleasantly surprised how willingly other newspapers will come to their aid. The assistance can range from identifying specific state laws that afford editors access to information to suggesting other avenues and approaches to flush out information.

■ Treat people with respect and sensitivity.

Individuals who expect to be drilled with tough questions immediately raise their radars when reporters approach. Yet they still need to be treated with respect.

The challenge is greater when the subjects are not accustomed to being in the public eye. Reporters will wind up with a better story if they ease into interviews and respect individuals' requests. Remember, these individuals — such as parents of victims at an accident scene — are under no obligation to say or volunteer anything. Reporters should be willing to give subjects some control of the situation. Delaying an interview for a few hours may mean no quotes for that day's paper, but it will make for a stronger story in the next edition.

Overaggressive reporters who badger individuals in these circumstances the same way they dog a city attorney are likely to wind up with nothing for a story. Worse yet, they have probably poisoned the reputation of the paper.

■ Be prepared.

Reporters may be armed with all the right questions. But are they prepared for uncooperative interviewees — no matter what the reason? There's often only one opportunity to get an interview.

Reporters who expect to be thrown into challenging circumstances should solicit tips from other reporters.

Some spot news events do not permit time to think through the process of getting a story from start to finish. That's why newsrooms, when developing policies for what to report about sensitive subjects, should give equal attention to developing approaches to getting the information.

Prepare for 'off the record' requests

Editors and reporters must be prepared to confront situations where individuals ask to speak "off the record." That's especially the case when writing about sensitive and challenging subjects.

Consider a tip from an assistant in City Hall who just typed a letter ratifying a severance agreement for a department head who is resigning under fire. Or consider a person who alerts the newspaper to the fact that a neighbor is going to volunteer his property as a potential landfill site.

It's a good bet that neither individual wants to attach his or her name to the initial public announcement of this news. Yet, both items are newsworthy and deserve to be made known to the broader community in a timely fashion.

These two examples also underscore a point common to many stories that result from the use of confidential sources: The information is likely public under most state data privacy laws. Besides, it's only a matter of time before a public body will formally release the information. A city council eventually will announce the department head's resignation, and a county board eventually will hold a public hearing on the best site for a new landfill.

Newspapers are doing their jobs, and gain more credibility, if they flush out and report the stories when they are timely — newsworthy — rather than letting authorities manage the news to their advantage.

Sources most often request to go "off the record." But reporters also must be prepared to negotiate requests by individuals to speak "on background" or "not for attribution."

"Off the record" usually means the information is for a reporter's understanding only. Reporters may leverage the knowledge to get other facts, but should not use the original information because to reveal it would compromise and might prove troublesome for the source.

"On background" usually means a newspaper may not use a source's name but may identify the person in terms of an organization — such as "a company source" or "a city official."

"Not for attribution" usually means specific information cannot be linked even indirectly to individuals because they might be identified. The story often might be reported, "This newspaper has learned … ."

The operative word in all of these definitions is "usually," which underscores the most important point for all concerned — that both reporters and sources must have a common understanding about the request. Sources might see nuances among the three variations, but the bottom line is their desire not to be linked to "breaking the story," especially if the information is deemed sensitive.

It's important that reporters not automatically stop an interview or resign themselves that they'll not get a story when such requests are made.

Reporters should not agree to anything immediately. Rather, they should continue the conversation to gain as much background as possible. At the end of the talk, they should review the information with the individual and see if some things can be attributed to them. One of the most persuasive arguments in stories of a "public" nature — something that will be acted upon by a public body in a public setting — is that the facts will be made known in any event. The public body and the newspaper both will gain credibility if they deliver the sensitive news as soon as it occurs.

It goes to the old good news/bad news scenario. City administration will call a local newspaper immediately upon learning it has received a significant federal grant for a civic project, even if the formal announcement will not be presented to the city council until its next meeting. But the details of employee discipline will not be released until a public body meets, even if the deal was struck a week earlier and the person is off the job.

Often, requests to go "off the record" — to withhold information until its official release — are made because the information has not been circulated internally among employees. For example, companies may not confirm employee layoffs because all affected individuals have not yet been notified. Or city administration may not have told all council members that an employee has been disciplined.

The argument by reporters to avoid going "off the record" — that the information will become public eventually — is more easily advanced when dealing with issues deemed public under state law. The termination of a public employee is a clear example.

But the reality is that the information — especially "unwelcome" news — spreads rapidly in all cases. In fact, a company's decision to lay off a hundred employees likely is more newsworthy and has far greater impact on a community than the discipline of a city department head. If a newspaper has received a tip, especially in small towns, there's a great likelihood that it's common knowledge on the street. Newspapers should work with key community individuals in both public and private sectors to make it "best practice" to release good and bad news as soon as possible.

The entire community will benefit from an honest and open exchange of all information, and newspapers likely will face fewer requests to go "off the record."

Chapter 10
Rights and responsibilities

The press has a right, and even an obligation in many cases, to print sensitive stories. The right and its accompanying responsibility are at the core of developing policies for reporting on sensitive issues.

In short, newspapers can be aggressive without being reckless. There is a difference in approaches, though the subjects of stories might not see it that way.

Four case studies from the *Red Wing Republican Eagle* underscore the types of decisions newsrooms routinely face. At issue is balancing the need to inform the public and the impact on the individuals involved.

In two cases, the newspaper delayed the reports at the request of authorities. In the two other cases, the newspaper proceeded with reports and drew criticism from those involved.

These arguments worked

In the first case, the newspaper delayed for nearly two months the report of a child stricken by E.coli bacteria. The primary concern was not to incite a health scare.

In the second case, the newspaper waited a week before reporting the kidnapping — and safe return — of a woman. The primary concern was the woman's safety.

Decisions to hold both stories were made after discussions with public officials and within the newsroom.

E.coli outbreak?

The E.coli episode began when someone alerted the newspaper that a child and a number of adults were infected with E.coli, and the child was hospitalized in serious condition. The individual also identified what was believed to be the source of the bacteria. The person gave no name or other details.

Another call came a couple of days later, asking why a case of E.coli had gone unreported and saying that another child was hospitalized with similar symptoms. Again, the caller left no name or details.

The news staff was not sitting idle. Staff followed up on both news tips and checked with the appropriate health-care services and the supposed source of the bacteria. The inquiries resulted in a flurry of calls among health officials, including one to the county task force that handled communicable diseases. Officials confirmed that a youth had been diagnosed with

E.coli, but it was unclear whether meat or contaminated flood water was the culprit.

Statistics also quickly put the case in perspective for the newsroom. The county routinely reported two to six isolated E.coli cases a year, and Minnesota identified 200 to 300 cases. The newsroom decided that a single case did not warrant a report.

Circumstances changed when the mother of the sick child asked how she could get her story published. Her purpose was to help warn others who might, as she did, mistake E.coli for a common sickness such as stomach flu. She also confirmed that meat was the source of the sickness. The resulting story informed residents about an important health issue.

As for the report that another child was being treated for E.coli? The Minnesota Department of Health reported nobody being treated for the bacteria in the local area. The newspaper received no additional calls after the article about the sick child was published.

Kidnapped woman returned unharmed

The kidnapping episode began with a call from local police — one week before the story hit the front page. The newspaper held the story even knowing that the FBI was assisting in the investigation. Family and friends feared for the life of the 21-year-old woman if her alleged kidnapper got word that authorities were on her trail.

The request to withhold the story was compelling in this case. The newspaper complied on the condition that the police chief would keep the family and newspaper abreast of developments. He did, and as soon as the woman was safe in custody, authorities released all of the details.

The newspaper still was first with the news. Readers were no worse off for having the story delayed a week, and any potential harm to the woman was averted.

These arguments didn't work

Editors should be sensitive to appeals to hold stories. Not all reasons are convincing, however. Indeed, holding news may not be in the best interest of the public, as exemplified in two other stories.

One dealt with another potentially serious health outbreak, and the other dealt with a judicial appointment gone awry.

Strep A outbreak

The *Red Wing Republican Eagle* was the first daily newspaper to break the story of an outbreak of invasive strep A bacteria, also known as the "flesh-eating" bacteria, in a nearby town. The newspaper believed the information was vital to readers, while also realizing that the story could create a scare.

State health officials did not share that opinion. The state epidemiologist conducted a press conference the same evening the story broke, confirming the outbreak. He issued two statements. One was a plea for calm among citizens. The other was an admonishment of the media for premature and inaccurate reports. He did not identify the *Republican Eagle* by name, but the newspaper was presumably part of the focus of his remarks.

Officials did not address, however, why it took so long to inform the public about what was going on.

The facts were that the Minnesota Department of Health first learned of the possible outbreak and began monitoring strep cultures on February 27. Laboratory tests showed that a single strain was responsible for four deaths and two illnesses during the weekend of March 11-12.

The story ran March 15, including comments from the victims' families. State officials did not confirm the outbreak until March 16.

The *Republican Eagle* was tipped off to the story by a two-paragraph article in a weekly newspaper announcing a press conference by the state epidemiologist to provide details on a toxic infection that had caused the deaths of four people. And the *Republican Eagle* had learned the previous day of an emergency meeting planned between county and state officials.

A call by a reporter to an area doctor confirmed the strep A outbreak, but no names were released due to patient confidentiality. Other newsroom personnel recalled the sudden and unexplained death of another area man a couple of months earlier.

The reporter did the rest, contacting a variety of people. One name led to another, and soon the newspaper identified all four local victims. Speculation that another death was linked to strep A proved unfounded, and that was reported the next day.

Newspapers must be sensitive to raising undue alarm, especially on something such as a potential disease outbreak. In the case of the invasive strep bacteria, the outbreak was confirmed prior to the first story by an area doctor and local health officials. The severity was established: four deaths. And suspicions about the unexplained deaths had been circulating in the nearby community.

The story was accurate. The only thing missing was an up-front acknowledgement by the Department of Health that all four deaths were linked to a single bacteria strain. Instead, state officials offered no comment until 24 hours after the story broke — when they confirmed the outbreak on their terms at a press conference.

Public health officials failed by not working with the press to get the information out immediately and accurately. That would have done more to calm citizens than waiting until people were alarmed by unexplained deaths and illnesses, and then telling them not to panic.

Judgeship stripped

A county prosecutor was the favorite to fill a judicial vacancy. Courthouse employees were so confident they purchased a congratulatory cake. The celebration, in May, was abruptly postponed that morning when the governor cited a scheduling conflict and canceled his trip to the city to announce the appointment.

The celebration was postponed permanently two weeks later when another attorney was appointed. The governor said the county prosecutor was "a wonderful candidate," but declined further comment. That appeared to be the end of the story until July, when the newspaper learned of an 11th-hour letter that had nixed the judgeship. A resulting investigation pieced together two critical pieces of the puzzle: a letter to the governor and a subsequent charge of sexual harassment. The story was published in August.

The report drew criticism on three fronts. The newspaper's decision on each front exemplified the difficult determinations often facing newsrooms. The failed judgeship clearly was news, but extenuating circumstances made it a sensitive story.

■ Why did the R-E wait until August — two weeks after filings closed for November elections and three months after the claims cost the county attorney a judgeship? (The attorney was running unopposed for another term as county prosecutor.)

The newspaper learned of the incriminating letter in mid-July, just days before election filings closed. The newspaper certainly had a right and obligation to tell constituents why the leading candidate was stripped of a judgeship. It also had a responsibility, however, to confirm the facts before putting a certain blemish on the attorney's record.

The newsroom immediately launched an investigation. The report was published two weeks later, when all the facts were verified.

■ Who leaked the story? Confidential sources should be used only if absolutely necessary. In this case, nearly 20 people were interviewed for the story. Some spoke on the record; some spoke off the record; some declined comment. The newspaper's guideline for using anonymous sources was that at least two people validate the information.

■ Why did the newspaper print the name of the complainant, an alleged victim of sexual harassment?

It's customary among most newspapers to not name victims of sexual abuse. There was a distinct difference in this case. For starters, the woman, a courthouse employee, complained of sexual harassment — not criminal sexual conduct.

This case was extraordinary in other regards:

■ The name was public knowledge because the complainant requested and received a leave of absence from her duties. Employees were openly speculating about her departure.

■ Allegations contained in her letter to the governor cost an individual his judgeship.

■ Her critical letter involved an elected official as well as the county's entire judicial system.

■ Counsel for the woman indicated early in the process that a civil suit would be forthcoming, at which time all information would be public. (The suit indeed was filed in October.)

In the end, the county and the complainant settled a six-figure, out-of-court settlement, and the county prosecutor was forced to resign.

Yes it's public, but be responsible

Newspapers' rights to publish a variety of information are supported by state and federal laws. Marriages and divorces; traffic tickets; hiring, firing, discipline, salaries and much more about public employees; court dispositions; bankruptcies; building permits; property taxes — these are just a sampling of public data.

But the fact that data are classified as public does not mean all readers welcome their dissemination. And authorities still may challenge the release of some data. Furthermore, the right to publish something is only half of the equation, as pointed out in the examples in this chapter. Newspapers also must be responsible in coverage, especially when dealing with sensitive issues.

Again, determining — and defending — that responsibility is fairly straightforward when, for example, stories involve public bodies and elected officials. Even in those cases, however, newspapers must consider such things as placement of story, balance and accuracy. Perceived unfair treatment of individuals or organizations will give newspapers a black eye.

Rights and responsibilities are less defined when tackling issues in the private arena. Readers will be less forgiving if they believe these individuals or organizations have been treated poorly in the press.

Timeliness is doubly important in reporting on sensitive issues. Delayed publication can unnecessarily aggravate a situation.

However, before newspapers get a shot at being punctual, they must receive the information from appropriate agencies. The process often has built-in delays. Newspapers have limited ability to speed up the process.

On the other hand, newspapers do have control over how soon the information gets published once it is received. All newspapers can improve turnaround.

Readers often ask why newspapers stand firm on access to and publication of a variety of records. It's much like the proverbial "if you give an inch, they'll take a mile." If the press agrees to one concession, all too often an individual or agency will try to stretch the rules. Soon laws are enacted with additional restrictions on what once was routinely public data — information that's important to readers.

Newspapers must stand solid on the belief that their communities — their readers — are best served by a full menu of public data rather than a selective serving.

More tips

Newspapers should weigh their rights and responsibilities in pursuit of all stories, but these considerations are especially important when reporting on sensitive issues. Here are some more tips:

■ Be accurate: If something cannot be confirmed, don't use it.

■ Be fair: If someone levels charges against an individual, seek a response from the accused.

■ Be consistent: If a story outlining alleged wrongdoing by someone appears on Page 1, and later the person is cleared, the follow-up story should get front-page treatment, too.

■ Be conscious of placement: If a story will receive just as much attention whether it's on Page 1 or Page 9, err on the side of playing the story inside.

■ Be prompt: If a story is linked to a sensitive event, and it is likely to be stressful on the subjects, be timely with reports. Be understanding of the impact of timing.

■ Be complete: If editors identify missing information in a story, readers will, too. An omission can be as damaging as misinformation.

■ Be knowledgeable: If an editor can't make sense of a story, most readers likely won't understand it either. Reporters must do their homework when writing about unfamiliar subjects.

■ Be sensitive: If a story strikes an editor as being sensational, readers will likely have a similar reaction. Pay attention to how stories are written, right down to word selection.

■ Be open to criticism: If readers are upset with newspaper policies, accept the feedback in forthright fashion. Don't squelch criticism. Use the opportunities to explain policies and/or to revisit and revise guidelines.

■ Be selective: If you're interviewing individuals unaccustomed to being in the public eye, choose quotes carefully. Stories should capture the flavor of an event, and reporters have no obligation to protect individuals by censoring, cleaning up or toning down what they say. At the same time, newspapers shouldn't go out of their way to put people in a bad or awkward light.

Chapter 11
Explaining newsroom decisions

Community newspapers play an essential role in the everyday lives of readers. Newspapers are the source of vital family happenings such as births and deaths. They report decisions of governing bodies and explain their impact on pocketbooks. They carry stories about student participation in school activities from speech and debate to theater and music to sports. They feature contributions of civic organizations. They provide coupons that offer discounts on products and services.

Newspapers deliver all of these things and much more. They also have guidelines about what they accept in all of these areas.

Readers often ask why something is or is not published. Many editors respond without hesitation, "Because that's the policy," offering little or no explanation.

Editors and publishers must make it a priority to explain news guidelines to readers as well as employees. It's doubly important when addressing tough and challenging issues.

Reporting on sensitive issues is a three-step process. Develop policies. Implement policies. Explain policies. The last step is arguably the most important part of the process.

Certain news events provide excellent opportunities to explain policies. But editors don't have to wait to begin a dialogue with readers. Policies can be discussed at any time. Periodic explanations help sharpen decision-making within newsrooms and reflect a willingness and commitment by newspapers to review guidelines and communicate with readers.

The reporting of some stories — the suicide of a popular youth, for example — is immediate fodder for explanatory columns. Newspapers cannot ignore the death, though the report will not be welcomed by everyone. Explaining the decision is important.

But numerous other policies — circumstances encountered weekly in newsrooms — warrant explanations, too. Many guidelines are considered the norm and taken for granted by editors and reporters, but they still can rankle readers, or at least prompt questions. For example: What are the limits on the number of words for letters to the editor, and why? What are the restrictions on photos that can be submitted for weddings, engagements and open houses, and why? What are the parameters for photos of check presentations, and why?

The list is endless. Even if editors never have to address a sensitive issue, all of these topics and more deserve an explanation to readers.

Three points are especially important in the explanation of policies.

■ Have the same person communicate policies. It's all right to acknowledge differences of opinion among staff, but one person should be the liaison to the community. Also, share policies with all newspaper employees.

■ Be open to feedback and criticism. Guidelines always should be subject to review. In the end, everyone may not agree with all policies. But the goal should be to help everyone better understand decisions.

■ Don't be afraid to admit mistakes or errors in judgment. A declaration by editors saying "we goofed" will go a long way toward earning respect and trust from readers.

Following are 12 columns from the *Republican Eagle* explaining newsroom policies.

Defining business news

News and advertising departments must operate closely, but independently. It's important to explain to businesses and readers alike the difference between what is a news story and what is a marketing promotion that should be advertised.

Our definition of business news
May 11, 1989

A restaurant gets new owners. That's news. The same restaurant sends out a press release about the popularity of its special home-made soup. That's an ad.

An investment firm relocates. That's news. The company announces a new line of annuities. That's an ad.

A retailer opens in town. That's news. The same merchant sends press releases about grand openings and successive anniversary sales. Those are ads.

All of these examples occurred in Red Wing and at nearly every other community newspaper. They point out one of the biggest misunderstandings which the R-E deals with daily: what's legitimately a news story, and what's strictly a promotion that should be advertised.

Weekly the R-E gets besieged with requests for "business news." Nearly every day some company promotes its wares through the mail. In almost every case, the advertising agencies know that what they're trying to pass off as a press release rightfully belongs in advertising columns.

All sorts of gimmicks

Agencies entice newspapers in every size and shape — literally.

Product samples routinely are delivered. At the R-E, most of these wind up alongside the accompanying press release in the wastebasket.

The R-E's business news is designated for exactly that — news. We report on new businesses, key changes such as a new location, new management or major remodeling, or a significant development in operations.

But we do not routinely report on changes which relate directly to marketing strategies. A new department, added product lines, internal staff reorganization, expanded services or reoccurring sales promotions with customer giveaways all properly fall under advertising.

Business briefs

Many business items are grouped under our "Business Briefs." Often these will be reports of employees attending seminars, achieving continuing education credits or professional designations, or being recognized for professional achievements.

We think that's important to share. It's similar to many of our "People" items which report of young men and women in the military service, or people being recognized for service to community organizations.

For businesses that do submit news releases, here's an important tip: Write the information in layman's language. Too often these items contain terminology and abbreviations more appropriate for a professional journal. The information may make perfect sense to fellow office workers, but — if left untouched by editors — the items would be Greek to most readers.

Editors often are stumped by the releases and have to make follow-up calls to make the message understandable to readers.

Independent departments

The news and advertising departments operate closely — but independently — at the *Republican Eagle*. If customers purchase an ad, they should expect professional and courteous service and a good return on their investments. But there is no link between how much advertisers spend with the R-E and how much news coverage their corresponding businesses receive.

Just as advertisers are entitled to courteous service by their R-E advertising representatives, they should expect and receive from the editor a courteous and clear explanation of the newspaper's separation between news and advertising.

Publishing public employee salaries

Newspapers have compelling reasons to publish the salaries of public employees. They should strive for consistency, though no system will be perfect.

Public salaries go with territory
January 18, 1990

Joe Johnson's thoughtful letter on this page set the editors to scratching their heads. Is it truly in the public interest to list the salaries of local government workers by name?

Johnson says he expects a certain "nakedness" as a city employee, but can't the *Republican Eagle*'s quest for public information be curbed at least a little in the interest of the privacy of individuals? Why not, for example, list the salary of the city chemist by position alone, eliminating the name of the job-holder?

Moreover, shouldn't the R-E be consistent and print the salaries of every public employee — union as well as non-union — at all levels of government?

We don't think the public is served by printing only titles and salaries. Secondly, the ideal situation would be to print all salaries. Both those are quick answers, and Johnson's letter deserves a more thorough exploration. Withholding names from the positions is at cross-purposes with our mission to provide information. In our book, that's nearly as bad as giving misinformation.

There are other complexities, such as being selective in whom we identify. We believe most people — except the individuals themselves — agree certain salaries should be published. For the city, the obvious ones include the council administrator, police chief, fire chief, city clerk, city engineer and public works director. In addition to holding supervisory positions, they in many ways participate in shaping city policy — how our tax dollars are spent.

No easy answers

If the R-E is selective in printing salaries, where should we draw the line? It's a difficult task. For example:

■ Print salaries of elected officials only. Is it fair to cite the county sheriff, who is elected, but not the city police chief, who is appointed?

■ Print salaries above a certain level. What's a fair figure — $20,000, $25,000, $30,000? It's far too subjective.

■ Print only supervisors. Again, it's too subjective. The standard also is flawed in cases where a non-supervisory employee — due to overtime — is paid more than a supervisor. Should those salaries be revealed, too?

One reason to print government salaries is to allow private employers to size themselves against the public sector. For the employee, the information might be a bargaining chip. For the employer, it shows how tough the competition is.

Given the arguments, the issue boils down to consistency: Either the R-E prints all the salaries or none at all. If we had the resources, we'd treat all government employees alike. For instance, is it right to print just school administrators' salaries — and not those of the 200-plus teachers whose incomes comprise 70 percent of the school budget?

Strive for consistency

Johnson presents an excellent challenge: The R-E should be as thorough with county or school wages as those for the city. We all must realize, though, that any policy will be second-guessed, and no system will be perfect.

Finally, publishing the wages falls under the category of protecting the rights the press has earned. Frequently, the R-E — and the press overall — is criticized for being a strong advocate of public information. There's a good reason for our effort. Each time public officials get a small opening, they take the proverbial mile. Consider two events of the past year:

■ Randy Erickson, former managing director of the municipal auditorium, was placed on probation in secrecy. The agenda — minus the personnel matter — was routine, so the R-E did not attend. The board took action and made no public disclosure until the issue was pressed.

■ Three members of a county board held an unscheduled session without announcing the intent to deal with social services issues, then quietly terminated the county's contract with its longtime mental health provider. Some other commissioners didn't even know about it until the issue surfaced a week later.

Johnson presents some excellent points. But just as he stands by his arguments, the R-E is resolved to keep public business public.

'Fair Play' policy

Fairness is at the crux of a newspaper's policy. Newspapers should endorse a Fair Play policy and regularly publish it. The *Red Wing Republican Eagle* welcomed readers to register their complaints with the Minnesota News Council.

Reader complains to News Council
July 11, 1991

"This newspaper tries conscientiously to report news fairly and accurately. When we fall short of this objective, we welcome complaints from our readers. Please direct your complaints to our editors whose names are listed here. If we cannot resolve our differences, we would welcome you to register your complaint with the Minnesota News Council, an organization which has our complete support."

The credo of the *Republican Eagle* — our Fair Play policy — is reprinted frequently on this page. We take complaints seriously. Fairness is at the crux of a newspaper's credibility.

A few weeks back, a reader pursued such a complaint regarding an R-E editorial. Although the reader wishes to remain anonymous, we believe others ought to know and understand the process.

The complaint never reached a hearing before the News Council, and no further action is planned. The issue was thoroughly discussed at our weekly news department meeting, however. The complainant's points were well taken. The press enjoys a powerful privilege in its editorial license. The complaint afforded an opportunity to review our editorial policy to identify how we can strengthen the process of researching and writing editorials.

Ground rules

A few steps and conditions are necessary before the News Council considers a case:

■ The complainant first must make an effort to settle the issue with newspaper management.

■ Since the newspaper would be asked ultimately to invest time and effort in responding to the complaint, the party must sign a waiver of future legal or administrative action on the same complaint.

■ If the complainant and newspaper are unable to resolve the issue, the council will consider a formal hearing. Both sides are invited to present their cases. The council votes either to deny or to uphold the complaint. A news release is sent to all media in the state. Just as in a court hearing, a minority opinion may be issued as well as the majority opinion.

■ The council typically rules on fairness within news stories. The News Council has decided there is a lot of leeway within editorial comment, particularly when public officials or figures are involved. They only get involved in editorial issues if facts are in dispute — opinions are neither right nor wrong.

At odds with editorial

The recent complaint involved an editorial which was characterized as unethical journalism. The chief issues raised were: The editorial expressed especially harsh criticism toward one individual; not all the facts were presented, as seen in the complainant's view, and therefore the editorial conclusions were tainted; this newspaper's editor had direct involvement in the issue, which the complainant believed was a conflict of interest.

The R-E's editorial board — including myself — met with the complainant to hear the concerns firsthand. We stood by our editorial position, but at the same time we sought to keep the lines of communication open so the reader would feel comfortable in contacting R-E management regarding any future concerns. We also offered our editorial page to the complainant to express the concerns. That offer was rejected.

Although the issues will not be detailed publicly, a couple of points regarding R-E editorial policy are important to note.

Unsigned editorials

The R-E indeed tries to avoid criticism of individuals. For the most part, we focus on public issues in terms of the responsible public body. But there are exceptions. If we deem individuals to be especially in the forefront of the issues, it is difficult not to single them out.

The issue of signing editorials, of stating when there is a personal involvement in an issue, is debated among readers and newspapers. It has resulted in many newspapers resorting to signed editorials only.

R-E editorials represent the view of this newspaper as an institution in this community. Although they are written primarily by one or two persons, they often represent collective opinion. Staff writers and others within R-E management routinely are consulted as opinions are formed.

In hindsight, the personal involvement perhaps should have been identified in the editorial in question. The involvement had been noted in an early news story about the issue, although much time had elapsed.

On the other hand, the R-E encourages employees and takes pride in the fact that our people are actively involved in the community. We believe it makes for a better newspaper as we keep in tune to the community pulse.

For that reason, our people are involved in a variety of civic activities — whether simply as volunteers or on formal commissions or boards. We could be adding footnotes to nearly any local editorial.

Keeping us alert

Minnesota stands alone in having a News Council. We believe wholeheartedly in the process.

We consider our editorial page the first resort for reader complaints. One of the primary roles of the letters column is to keep the R-E on its toes. Rarely have readers been afraid to tell us what they think; we hope they continue to keep us on target.

Advertiser treatment

Newspapers should be sensitive to the concerns of all customers/readers, but the same standards should be applied to all. In the long run, everyone benefits from a policy of clear separation between news and advertising.

No privileges for advertisers
March 18, 1993

"You won't read that in the paper," the person says. "After all, it's one of the R-E's biggest advertisers."

That comment might hold truth at some newspapers, but it's not the case here. Over the years we've probably frustrated more than a few advertisers who seek privileges getting something printed in or omitted from the newspaper.

We pride ourselves on the distinction between news and advertising. In the long run, everyone benefits from a policy of clear separation.

Vital to newspaper

The R-E's experiences with advertisers likely are mirrored in a study recently released by Marquette University in Milwaukee.

The survey revealed that advertisers have pressured more than 90 percent of U.S. newspapers to change or kill stories. On a positive note, only one-third of the newspapers caved into those pressures.

Rejecting an advertiser's request is not an easy decision at all newspapers, especially in smaller operations. An advertiser may well decide to boycott the newspaper, which — in some cases — could cause significant impact.

Advertising obviously is vital to this newspaper. But it's the combination of advertising and news that gives the product its overall value. Neither can succeed without the other.

Individual merits

We get our share of cases where someone attempts to use his or her pull to get an event covered. The same pressures can be applied to quash an item, especially if it might be embarrassing to the business.

We're sensitive to the concerns of any reader/customer. But if we're to maintain credibility, we must apply the same standards to all.

Each request is judged on its individual merits, no matter who the person may be.

Describing violence

Newspapers should strive to give readers a true picture of violence and still take pains to protect the victims. The two missions often collide.

Challenges of reporting violence
April 29, 1993

The murder of Charlene Swanson last month has raised the awareness of domestic abuse one more notch in this community. Yet it's one of the most difficult subjects we cover in the newspaper — due both to legal restrictions and to our concern for all the parties involved.

Our reporter's excellent package a week ago gave insight into what it's like to be the victim of domestic abuse. We hope the stories also gave other victims of domestic violence timely information about where they can turn for assistance.

For her own safety, the woman interviewed remained anonymous. This need to be nameless underscores one of the many challenges in reporting violent crimes, especially domestic offenses. We strive to give readers a true picture of violence, yet at the same time take pains to protect the victims.

Missions collide

The two missions often collide.

Most crimes are reported by the R-E in rather straightforward fashion. The incident is noted, listing both the complainant and the accused.

But special rules are applied when reporting physical and sexual violence. Details typically are withheld from publication, in deference to victims. Indeed, we purposely camouflage reports of interfamilial abuse, sticking strictly to terminology citing first-degree sexual abuse, second-degree abuse, etc.

That policy change was made several years ago in direct response to concerns by social services professionals. Their reasoning is logical and we believe reflects the general community attitude: Spare the victim additional public embarrassment. Friends of the victim and those in the legal network realize the seriousness of the charges. Others need not know each and every detail.

At the same time, by protecting the victim, we don't give everyone an accurate picture of the circumstances or the level of crime in the community. It can be argued reasonably that more explicit reporting could raise red flags for people in similar predicaments.

Rights of accused

Not to be lost in the overall picture is protection of those who have been accused but not convicted. Domestic abuse is one of the most horrendous crimes and often leads to public outcry for vigilante justice in the way of the Old West.

Due process of the law is probably even more critical in violent crimes such as domestic and physical abuse. Rights of the accused are especially important when the accusation is most inflammatory. The U.S. judicial system still is based on the premise that a person is innocent until proven guilty.

It's unfortunate, but the intricacies — legal and otherwise — of domestic violence hinder coverage of the problem. Indeed, local law enforcement authorities reported several calls from metropolitan media on hearing about the murder of Swanson. But once told that domestic abuse likely was involved, they didn't pursue the story.

We remain interested in drawing attention to violent crime. But the circumstances of domestic and physical abuse place them in a special category.

Tragic photos

Readers were quick to criticize a front-page photo showing a grieving mother upon learning her son had committed suicide. Editors should readily accept opposing viewpoints — and criticism when it's warranted — but should reject the blanket charge of sensationalism.

Photo 'told' the tragedy
February 10, 1994

Readers were loud and clear about last week's coverage of a high-speed chase which resulted in the death of an 18-year-old from a neighboring community. They told us we had no business running a front-page photo, showing the grieving mother upon learning her son had committed suicide.

Several comments were published in People's Platform, and I responded to each reader individually. I also spoke with Joan Larson, the mother, who expressed her anger over the photo being printed.

All readers deserve the same explanation.

The Feb. 3 incident was very much a public event. Several officers and half a dozen enforcement agencies were involved in the five-hour ordeal that included a high-speed chase. An officer came dangerously close to being run over. Randy Larson, the victim, had a history of trouble with the law.

Our pursuit was far from a deliberate intrusion into a private situation. Indeed, had we known from the beginning it was a suicide, we probably would not have gone to the scene.

The R-E was alerted at 6:45 a.m. on the police scanner to what was perceived to be a standoff. As it turned out, Larson already was dead. But from the information at hand, it sounded like a potential hostage situation.

Our news editor/photographer found squad cars and officers everywhere, but no one was readily available for firsthand information. As he rounded one of the vans, he saw the women — their backs to the camera. As they turned around, he snapped the photograph.

They had just been told of the suicide.

But our photographer still did not know and figured the mother was distraught over her son trapped in the house. Only after she got into an ambulance, and others dispersed, did an officer alert our photographer to the details.

Publication of the photo, admittedly difficult on the family and friends, caught the essence of the tragedy. The mother had come, she said, thinking that her son probably was dead but still ready to talk to him. Her worst fears were realized.

The decision to print the photo was not a snap judgment. We discussed it in detail.

Some readers have charged sensationalism. We readily accept opposing viewpoints — and criticism when it's warranted — but we reject the blanket charge. The R-E, in contrast with the television industry, is quite sensitive regarding graphic photos and descriptive text.

But our job is to report the news — good and bad. Violence and grief are very much a part of our everyday lives. In this case, we deemed it appropriate to picture the tragic moment, but we do not disregard the fact that there are strong differences of opinion.

Crime coverage

The R-E's treatment of the stabbing epitomizes the difficulty and sensitivity that all newspapers face in reporting crime, and especially in high-profile cases such as stabbings. It goes to the heart of the debate over free press/fair trial.

R-E falls short in stabbing case
December 18, 1997

A reader asked Wednesday in People's Platform: "Why do some people's stories make front-page news and then when other people's side of the story comes out, it's printed on the second or third page? Is there a reason for this or a bias as far as the paper goes?"

The caller referred to Tuesday's report in which a female eyewitness to a stabbing Oct. 26 cleared the victim of any wrongdoing. The Tuesday article appeared on page 2. Her statement was significantly different than her earlier account which was published on page 1.

The female eyewitness account, in an Oct. 28 article, stated that the stabbing occurred when her fiancé, male 1, saw the victim, male 2, attempting to force her to have sex. Charges were filed against male 1. The article appeared across the front page.

The caller is correct. The follow-up should have been published on page 1 as well, especially considering the significance of the eyewitness statements. The decision to place the article on page 2 was not sufficiently thought through and fell short in terms of fair play.

Our treatment of the stabbing epitomizes the difficulty and sensitivity that all newspapers face in reporting crime, and especially in high-profile cases such as stabbings. It goes to the heart of the debate over free press/fair trial.

Criminal complaints, by law, are public records. It seems appropriate to publish some of the details that substantiate the charges leveled against a person.

The difficulty lies in the fact that complaints often contain no rebuttal from the accused. That may not come until the trial or negotiations between attorneys, which could be months after the incident.

The Red Wing stabbing was even more complex. First, the victim, male 2, did not face charges, but admittedly was put in a poor light by the initial account. Secondly, he was hospitalized at the same time the charges were filed against male 1 and could not give a statement to police.

Several people called when we first reported the stabbing, saying the report was one-sided. We declined publishing their comments. It is our policy not to "try" a case in the newspaper.

But we assured them that once the victim, male 2, gave a statement to the police, we'd print his side of the story.

We've yet to receive the victim's version of the incident, but obviously the statement of the female eyewitness was powerful. It deserved more prominent placement.

We've apologized to the victim, assuring him that as the case progresses and the facts are released, we'll give those articles proper attention.

Confidential sources

Many believe that the use of sources "speaking on the condition of anonymity" is overused among the Washington press corps. Too much secretiveness can threaten the credibility of newspaper reports. But there comes a point — in some important stories — when it's necessary to offer confidentiality in exchange for critical information.

Protecting confidential sources
January 29, 1998

In May 1994, County Attorney Jerry Smith was the odds-on favorite to be selected for a judgeship. The governor withdrew the appointment following an 11th-hour letter written by Smith's former office manager, Amy Ryan.

The *Republican Eagle* was able to provide detailed accounts of the unraveling of the appointment, thanks to a confidential source. The story was of utmost public interest as it escalated into a sexual-harassment lawsuit filed by Ryan against Smith and the county. Nearly 18 months later, the county paid Ryan $185,000 in an out-of-court settlement.

The R-E was protected from revealing its source and all of its unpublished materials. The case was filed in federal court, and the R-E enjoyed the safeguard of the federal shield law.

It could well have been a different scenario, had Ryan's civil suit been filed in a state court. Minnesota has a law which protects secret sources, too, but the protection of unpublished notes has been extremely weakened by court rulings in recent years.

The Smith case is an excellent argument as to why the Minnesota Legislature should bolster protection of confidential materials for journalists. In short, state law should be consistent with federal law.

Even with the federal law, R-E reporters were challenged in court to identify the newspaper's source and produce unpublished notes. The judge ruled in our favor.

State legislation

A bill has been introduced to restore the state law to what the Legislature originally intended. It passed the Senate Judiciary Committee and is headed for the full body. A companion bill has yet to be heard in the House.

Journalists fear that the present law — left unchanged — will hinder news gathering. The concern is real. In fact, a local law enforcement officer said he watched closely when the R-E was being pressed by Ryan's attorney to reveal our source and unpublished notes.

Had the judge ruled against the R-E, the officer said he and others would rethink seriously how much information they are willing to share with reporters. It's fairly common for authorities to offer background information or keep us apprised of cases. In the end, it gives the public a more complete picture.

In the Smith case, the civil suit did acknowledge the 11th-hour letter sent by Ryan. But the information was revealed weeks after our original report, and the details of the letter never would have been made public had it not been for our source.

Sources, notes

It's important to note that journalists are not asking for any privileges that are not already guaranteed under federal law.

As a rule, we avoid publishing stories based solely on confidential material. Even the Smith story was based on interviews with a number of individuals, many of whom were identified.

Indeed, we believe that the use of sources "speaking on the condition of anonymity" is overused among the Washington press corps. Too much secretiveness can threaten the credibility of a report.

But there comes a point — in some important stories — when it's necessary to offer confidentiality in exchange for critical information. The readers are the ultimate winners by getting a full set of facts.

The Red Wing officer's comments underscore the importance of the issue. Yes, existing state law offers protection of confidential sources, but not of unpublished notes. The distinction is not very comforting to sources when they know a reporter is being subpoenaed — even if it's solely to produce notes. Wary that their identities might be revealed, they simply stop talking.

How much information?

Newspapers have a responsibility to inform the public about serious issues, especially those that can affect health and safety. But there is a fine line regarding how much information is presented.

Report on meth lab valuable to dialogue
February 10, 2000

Did the *Republican Eagle* overstep its bounds in reporting on the police raid of an apparent methamphetamine lab last week?

A reader took the Feb. 2 report to task in People's Platform last Friday. He commented, in part, "I thank you for making available to residents — especially the youth of Red Wing — this excellent investment opportunity. Who'd have thought that for just $150 and a little fertilizer off the farm, I could make $2,000 in just two hours work? Why would anyone want to raise cows? And we're providing a needed service. After all, as the article stated, meth is the drug of choice."

This newspaper has a responsibility to inform the public about serious issues, especially those that can affect health and safety. But we acknowledge there also is a fine line regarding how much information is presented. The reader's call is a reminder that we continually review how we address such subjects as alcohol and drug abuse.

We believe that in this case the article played a role in educating residents on the dangers of this drug and its growing presence in our communities. In hindsight, the article could have gone further in detailing the health hazards of using "meth."

Community dialogue

We're not alone in our assessment. We used the reader's comments as a springboard to quiz professionals in the business of drug counseling and enforcement.

Josh Ritchie, social worker at Red Wing High School, said he viewed the news story as an opportunity to be proactive and offer education on the subject.

"It's important to have the dialogue," he said, as opposed to being in denial about the fact that meth labs are a problem here. Ritchie challenged the suggestion that the newspaper report could lead youths to make methamphetamine. In reality, he said, kids can log onto the Internet and find out just about anything — from making bombs to chemicals.

Ann Swanson, nurse for Red Wing Schools, said she doubted the article would motivate kids to experiment with the drug; youths inclined to do so aren't seeking information from the R-E.

"I think it helps warn the parents that they should watch for this," Swanson said.

She also pointed to the public safety issue — that meth labs pose tremendous fire hazards due to the chemical fumes and heat sources used including small burners and propane torches.

Swanson compared the reader's criticism of reporting about drug labs to those people who are critical of the school's sex education program. They charge that teaching sex education only encourages promiscuity.

Public safety

Chet Maddox, environmental health director for Goodhue County, viewed the report from the perspective of public safety.

"It's not only an issue of breaking the law by making drugs, but it's also a safety issue for those in the area," he said. Meth labs are a fire hazard. "It goes to a bigger issue."

Eric Armstrong, Goodhue County chief deputy, also endorsed efforts to provide information about the increasingly easy access to methamphetamine. People must be made aware of the dangers.

"Unfortunately, meth has become a drug of choice among young people," he said. Yet most young people have no idea of the damaging effects of the drug.

There is a point at which newspaper reports could go too far, he said — such as offering specific recipes to make the drug.

At the same time, Armstrong questioned whether the report went far enough. When discussing methamphetamine, it's important to explain fully the harshness and the danger of the chemical to those individuals who use it.

Knowledge vs. ignorance

In the final analysis, he said, knowledge is power — no matter what the subject. "The more you know, the better off you are," Armstrong said. "Unfortunately, some people believe that ignorance is best."

The reader's reaction did not surprise Armstrong. He'll often be challenged by parents about the amount of information he provides during presentations on drugs to youths.

"You shouldn't go into anything without proper knowledge," he said. "At least then you can make an educated decision."

Privacy vs. right to know

The heroes in this lifesaving story of a 7-week-old boy included his foster parents, who were identified. The boy's name purposely was absent. In this case, editors decided the potential hurt to the natural parent out-weighed the public's right to know the identity of the infant.

This time, privacy outweighs right to know
March 2, 2000

Our front page Monday carried a report of a 7-week-old boy who was revived after suffering cardiac arrest. The "heroes" included foster parents John and Sarah Robinson of Red Wing along with Lt. Randy Smith who was first to arrive at the house. Scott Jackson, Randy Olson and Doug Rogers also were among those who responded.

One name was purposely absent from the article — the name of the child, who was under foster care. We also didn't publish the child's name in the ambulance runs printed on the FYI page.

In this case, we decided the potential hurt to the natural parent outweighed the public's right to know the identity of the infant. We made the decision after speaking with personnel at Social Services.

The *Republican Eagle* has a strong tradition of aggressive reporting. In most cases, if information is a public record, it is published.

But the right to publish public records carries an accompanying responsibility. On rare occasions, we'll withhold information. This was one of those cases.

Our reticence stemmed from the fear that one or more of the child's parents might be living in the area. Identifying the child, who was born with medical problems, would raise the obvious question among acquaintances of the family: Why was the boy not in his parents' home?

Welfare Director Sam Jacobson confirmed our suspicion. In nearly all cases foster children are placed with families in the home county. That was true here as well; one of the youth's natural parents lives in this county.

In the final analysis, we asked ourselves whether we still had a compelling story without identifying the child.

As Jacobson said, "It was a great story. They (the crew) did a terrific job."

We continue to be vigilant regarding public information and the needs of readers. As always, though, we base decisions on the merits of each case.

Family shares story

A local family shared the story of their son, who committed suicide, in an attempt to help the community address a hidden problem that affects many people. They have shown us all that it is possible to use even the worst of circumstances as a positive force for ourselves and society.

Rileys turn tragedy into a positive forum
December 26, 2002

The *Republican Eagle* will present its top local stories of 2002 in a commemorative edition next week. The event rated No. 1 was an overwhelming selection: the financial challenges facing the Red Wing School District. The aftermath of the failed referendum this month underscores that the teachers' strike left many divisions; the community faces a long healing process.

Included in the top 10 stories is an especially noteworthy one, however. The suicide of Larry Riley — son of Doug and Diane and brother of Robin — resonated not only among his family and friends, but throughout Red Wing. The Rileys had lost another son, Sam, five years earlier in a car accident.

The Rileys shared Larry's story in an attempt to help the community address a hidden problem that affects many people. As they said in August, "Suffering without meaning is a tragedy."

They underscored the importance of talking openly about their son's illness — depression. Their public response in dealing with a personal tragedy prompted an outpouring of community support.

The Riley story was important for another reason. Larry Riley's death put the spotlight on a significant social issue. The story also did not end with his death. The Riley family used a portion of memorial gifts to sponsor a forum on depression and suicide. More than 500 people came to the Sheldon Theatre to listen to a program arranged with the help of the Goodhue County chapter of the National Association of Mental Illness.

The elections had just finished, which changed Minnesota's political landscape. The community was embroiled in the teachers' strike. But residents put those things aside to talk about a "silent" illness. The forum emphasized that the need to address social issues is just as important as the attention paid to taxes and public safety if we are to maintain a healthy community.

The Riley story sends another message that we all can strive for in 2003: to seek a balance between the good and the bad, to recognize what is positive instead of always focusing on the negative — without being Pollyannas.

Doug, Diane and Robin Riley have shown us all that it is possible to use even the worst of circumstances as a positive force for ourselves and society.

Chapter 12
Sample policies

Newspapers often take disparate approaches to similar stories. Differences can be especially striking among small weeklies or dailies and their big-city counterparts.

There is no correct way to report a story, and that's why all newspapers should have written guidelines for news coverage. Policies don't always offer black-and-white answers to a predicament, but they do offer a deliberative process to reach decisions.

Policies should set the ground rules, and they must be flexible. For example, it may be standard procedure to acknowledge the suspension of high school athletes in a game story, and then put the matter to rest. But what if a suspension costs a team a tournament title? The disciplinary action — normally a two-sentence notation — is elevated to headlines.

This chapter includes sample policies for a variety of news items. Some circumstances, such as suicides, will be encountered on an infrequent basis. Other policies, such as those regarding weddings and obituaries, are dealt with regularly.

Each newspaper must go through its own process to tailor policies to local communities. The following policies should be viewed as a starting point for those discussions. And talking with people — individuals inside and outside the newspaper — is arguably the most important aspect of developing policies. The more opinions that are solicited, the stronger the policies will be.

Accidents

Premise
Accidents, especially those involving serious injuries or fatalities, are among the staples of community news. Accidents frequently are of a very public nature, especially when the scenes disrupt traffic.

Parameters
■ Photos of accident scenes — but not necessarily the victims — are news.

■ Avoid publication of gruesome photos. To be specific, do not publish photos which show body parts of victims or pools of blood.

■ Be sensitive to photos that show outlines of bodies, even if they are covered. These photos may be appropriate to use, but covered bodies, in general, should not be the focal point of photos.

■ Understand that every victim has a life story. Track down and report the life stories of victims with as much vigor as you use to get a photo of their last moments of life. Search for other photos — even if only a mug shot — to use in these stories.

■ Reactions of bystanders — though often a good photo opportunity — might require sensitivity, too, especially if bystanders are immediate family members.

■ Some images of accident scenes are best described in text.

■ A checklist of items should be standard protocol for all accident stories that result in serious injuries and/or deaths. Were all vehicle occupants wearing seat belts? Were motorcycle drivers/passengers wearing helmets? Were tickets issued? Was the influence of drugs/alcohol a factor? What were weather and road conditions?

Consistency

Newspapers cannot be at the scene of all accidents. Photo coverage is haphazard by the nature of circumstances. But newspapers can be consistent in the subject matter of photos and the information included in stories.

Communication

Law enforcement authorities must be aware of newspaper policies for accident coverage, especially in terms of coverage at the scenes. Authorities often are reluctant to permit reporters and/or photographers near the site and may even try to prohibit them from talking with anyone. Reporters also have a responsibility to conduct themselves in a professional manner. Fewer confrontations will occur if both sides sit down and agree on ground rules in advance. This should be done with any agency the newspaper may come in contact with — including local police, county sheriffs and state patrols.

Business news

Premise

News about businesses — large and small — is news about friends and neighbors and has great meaning. Businesses are a source of employment and often contribute to local quality of life through philanthropy and employer/employee involvement. Distinctions must be made, however, between what is legitimate news and what is marketing.

Parameters

■ Business openings — but not necessarily grand openings — are news. Store openings should be reported on a timely basis. Grand openings only warrant coverage if they are done simultaneously with the actual opening.

■ Photos should focus on the principals of the business, and not the mayor, chamber of commerce ambassadors, or other community representatives who routinely perform ceremonies at store openings.

■ Certain anniversaries should be consistently covered — i.e., 25 years, 50 years, 75 years, 100 years. Guidelines should be in place for these benchmark anniversaries. For example, 25-year observances likely warrant a story and photo on an inside page. Fifty years and more might warrant front-page coverage. Stories should be substantive, and not focus on the accompanying marketing event. Other anniversaries generally should be promoted through paid advertising.

■ Groundbreaking photos are the exception rather than the rule. They should be limited primarily to public projects and significant private projects.

■ Businesses routinely give money to a variety of community and private projects — whether an annual contribution to a booster club or one-time participation in a capital drive for a hospital expansion. It's impractical to recognize all of these contributions, and in most cases publicity should be limited to the one-time donations. Newspapers must set guidelines, recognizing that a $100 contribution for some companies is just as noteworthy as $1,000 for others.

■ Make a distinction between business news and business promotion. Relocations, expansions and management changes are properly the subject of news stories. New product lines, new store hours and customer sweepstakes winners should be promoted through paid advertising.

■ Business closings and work stoppages are news, too. Newspapers must report "good" and "bad" news.

■ Print business items in layman's language. Business news often includes terminology and abbreviations more appropriate for professional journals.

■ Newspapers should make no link between how much advertisers spend and how much coverage their businesses receive.

■ Trust between writers and news sources is imperative, but especially so when issues involve profits and livelihood. In certain circumstances, newspapers may agree to a confidential briefing by a business with an agreed-upon release date for the information.

Consistency

Business news must be judged on objective guidelines, and not on how much an advertiser contributes to a newspaper's bottom line. Publishers especially must subscribe to and defend this policy. News value should be the major criteria in deciding when an event warrants coverage. That's in the best interests of everyone — advertisers and readers alike.

Communication

Internal and external communications are equally important when outlining guidelines for business news. Newspaper advertising representatives should have a clear understanding of what is accepted as business news. Policies also can be conveyed directly to businesses through such avenues as invoices.

Confidential sources

Premise

The use of confidential sources erodes the credibility of newspapers, especially when they are the source of news considered "unwelcome" by most readers.

Parameters

■ As a general rule, avoid publishing stories based solely on confidential material. Confidential sources should be used as a last resort to get a story and/or information vital to a story.

■ Confidential sources are not the same as anonymous sources. Newspapers must know the name of informants, even if the names are not published in connection with a specific story.

■ Editors should authorize use of all confidential sources, prior to reporters making any agreements with the sources.

■ Information supplied by a confidential source must be confirmed by at least one other source before it is used.

■ Background information — not directly attributed to an individual — is an accepted practice in order to produce a more complete story.

Consistency

The use of confidential sources among the Washington press corps underscores why these sources should be the exception rather than the rule. Open the door to the use of anonymous sources, and they become the norm. Soon no one will speak on the record.

Communication
All reporters should be instructed as part of their job orientation that the use of confidential sources is discouraged, if not prohibited.

Election coverage

Premise
Election coverage — from start to finish — is among the most demanding of newsroom tasks. Spell out as many aspects of coverage as possible, as the pace will become chaotic as elections approach.

Parameters
■ List all races that need to be covered — from local to state to federal. Be sure to include local or state referendums.

■ Identify key dates — endorsement conventions, filing periods, primary and general elections.

■ Determine how candidacies will be announced. Will incumbents and challengers/newcomers be treated the same?

■ Assign reporters to specific races.

■ Prepare for candidate interviews. Reporters must be knowledgeable about issues. Quiz candidates on similar issues, where appropriate.

■ Decide how much attention, if any, the newspaper will give to statewide races. Have a plan for coverage of statewide candidates who make campaign stops in your community.

■ Decide on the format for candidate interviews — i.e. profiles, sidebars, Q&A, written questionnaires, photos. Different reporters will have different writing styles, but the presentation of the information should be similar.

■ Candidate profiles should get consistent play. Articles on opposing candidates ideally should be in the same edition on the same page.

■ Identify criteria for covering debates. Consider the sponsors. Consider the timing of debates with respect to other newspaper coverage.

■ Decide how to report candidate endorsements by other candidates and special-interest groups. "Media events" usually should receive low priority.

■ Incumbents and challengers are likely to issue press releases. It's important that stories include a response from the other candidates, especially if charges have been leveled.

■ Be alert to races that demand special attention — e.g., a candidate who loses the party's endorsement but wins the primary election; high-profile and expensive campaigns (lots of advertising); visible campaigning by incumbents for other candidates in local elections; special-interest support for non-partisan offices.

■ Be consistent in photo coverage of campaigns.

■ Post and package election stories on Web sites for easy reference.

■ Publish a complete lineup of races prior to election day, mirroring the ballot that voters will get at the polls. List polls and times.

■ If a Voters Guide is published, decide what to include in the guide and what to include in the regular paper.

■ Pay attention to the timing of all coverage — news stories as well as editorial endorsements — so there is adequate opportunity for reader comments and rebuttals on the editorial page.

■ Scrutinize letters submitted as part of a letter-writing campaign. Mass-produced letters — even if submitted by local residents — should be rejected.

Consistency

Every aspect of election coverage — from candidate profiles to debates to editorial endorsements to treatment of letters to the editor — is put under the microscope, especially if readers perceive newspapers to have a political bias. It matters little whether that perception is limited to the editorial page. Most readers do not make a distinction between the editorial page and news stories.

Communication

The whys and hows of election coverage cannot be communicated enough to candidates and readers. Why are some debates covered and not others? Why do newspapers endorse candidates, and what are the criteria? Are there limits on letters to the editor? Editors should seize the opportunity to explain policies to readers during each election cycle.

Letters to the editor

Premise

Letters to the editor — the exchange of ideas — are the lifeblood of editorial pages and the heart of newspaper vitality. Newspapers should encourage letters, emphasizing letters by local residents on local issues.

Parameters

■ Letters should be limited to 350 words.

■ Individuals should be limited to one letter per month, except in the case of rebuttals (see next item).

■ Letters might prompt rebuttals. Exchanges should be limited to two letters from each individual on a particular subject — in other words, a letter and a rebuttal, plus a counter-rebuttal from each writer.

■ In general, letters should be accepted from local readers only. An exception might be a letter on a local topic from a recognized expert who lives outside the area.

■ Mass-produced letters — even if submitted by a local resident — should be rejected.

■ All letters must be verified prior to publication, preferably by a phone call.

■ "Thank you" letters generally are not accepted, especially those that list each individual who contributed to the success of an event.

■ Letters submitted as part of a letter-writing campaign will be scrutinized, especially those submitted during election season.

■ The same guidelines that apply to letters in the newspaper apply to online letters.

■ Be sensitive to the prominence letters receive — how they are displayed — especially those that present opposing views on the same issue.

■ Make readers aware that letters are edited aggressively, especially those that repeat themes.

■ Letters should carry an editor's note identifying the writer if it's germane to the letter. For example, a writer might be identified as a nuclear engineer if the letter addresses a nuclear energy issue. Individuals writing in support of a candidate should be identified if they are campaign activists.

■ Letters should be restricted to public issues or issues that come before public bodies. Compliments and/or criticism of private organizations and businesses are not regular subjects for letters.

Consistency

Editors must be consistent in how they edit and display letters, especially when dealing with letters that address opposing viewpoints of an issue.

Communication

Newspapers should regularly publish their policy on letters to the editor, underscoring that all letters are subject to editing. Readers are especially possessive of letters. They believe that since they are the author, not a word should be changed.

Local editorials

Premise
The exchange of ideas is at the heart of a vibrant newspaper and community. Newspapers cannot fulfill that role unless they regularly offer opinions on local issues.

Parameters
■ Editorials are one of the best examples of newspapers displaying community leadership.

■ It's easy to be a booster of projects with broad-based support. Those editorials should not be overlooked. But responsible newspapers also must tackle issues that are dividing a community.

■ Editorials are most balanced, and thus strongest, when they identify strengths and weaknesses of both sides of an issue, and then offer a resolution or conclusion.

■ Editorials generally should stick to issues, and not personalities. That's an especially important point when endorsing candidates in local elections, which often become personality contests.

■ Newspapers should not shy away from making election endorsements, especially in local races. Editorials can offer singular insight to candidates.

■ Editorials require the highest standards of accuracy in reporting. Editorial positions should not be skewed on the basis of whether they might anger major advertisers or prominent individuals.

■ Editorials are based on facts, and those facts must be stated. In the end, however, editorials must offer an opinion.

■ Editorials should state any conflicts of interest — by the newspaper or its employees.

Consistency
The most credible editorial pages are those that remain consistent in positions, no matter the pressure they receive to change their stances. However, newspapers should not be afraid to rethink positions if warranted by new information that surfaces.

Communication
Newspapers should regularly educate readers on the role of an editorial page. In general, editors should communicate with readers how editorials are distinct from news stories. Editors should take advantage of specific opportunities, such as explaining the newspaper's role in political endorsements.

Obituaries

Premise

Deaths are reported in a variety of ways — from paid death notices to routine obituaries to deaths that are front-page news.

Parameters

■ For paid notices, individuals provide and pay for the exact wording of the obituary. Newspapers still should review the copy to ensure it is tasteful and does not raise any red flags — such as potential legal action.

■ News judgment must be exercised in the case of prominent individuals and others whose deaths warrant separate stories. Reporters pursue these the same as any other assignment, making decisions on who to interview and what information to include. Colorful details in a news story are not only acceptable but desirable.

■ A third category — news obituaries — can fall into two groups. Some newspapers will choose to write news obituaries about select individuals, either because they were prominent or because they led interesting lives. At other newspapers — where the number of deaths is manageable — staff reporters write news obituaries for everyone.

In both cases, reporters review and report facts from information provided by families. The practice allows subjectivity and freedom to carry more detail on certain aspects of individuals' lives. But newspapers still should have guidelines for news obits.

Among the guidelines:

◆ Obituaries must have a local connection — however that is determined. The clearest connection is local survivors. The deceased also may have been known to many people through their profession or some other presence.

◆ Establish deadlines to ensure obituaries can be reported in a timely fashion.

◆ Write obituaries in a standard format. Flowery language will not be accepted.

◆ Cause of death will not be reported in an obituary unless requested by the family.

◆ Up to three hobbies/interests of the deceased will be noted.

◆ Names of survivors will be limited to: parents; brothers and sisters and any spouses; sons and daughters and any spouses. "Stand-alone" in-laws will not be listed unless they are the only local survivor.

◆ Requests for identifying special friends, caregivers, etc. among the survivors are evaluated on an individual basis.

◆ Individual names of grandchildren or great-grandchildren are not listed among survivors. Obituaries simply will list the numbers.

◆ Pallbearers will be limited to eight names. Honorary pallbearers will be limited to 16 names, recognizing that many families will list grandchildren and great-grandchildren as honorary pallbearers as a way to recognize them.

◆ Color or black-and-white photos will be accepted, but all photos will be reproduced in black-and-white. No photos of individuals will be accepted that are more than 20 years old.

◆ No obituaries will be accepted without the name and contact information of the person submitting the information.

Consistency
Obituaries are a foundation of community news. Families and funeral homes scrutinize death notices to make sure everyone receives equal treatment.

Communication
Obituary policies should be published regularly in the newspaper. They also should be distributed through such places as funeral homes and churches.

Proclamations

Premise
Proclamations in and of themselves are not news, and usually are an artificial avenue to produce attention. Proclamations are so commonplace that there's one for just about every cause imaginable.

Parameters
■ Publicize proclamations only when they are connected with a local event.

■ Focus of stories/photos should be the work of the group/event being recognized, and not on those issuing the proclamation. For example, draw attention to Week of the Child-Care Provider by interviewing a local provider, not by publishing a photo of a mayor signing a proclamation.

■ Proclamations typically recognize organizations that do year-round work. Newspaper coverage should not be restricted to specific days, weeks or months — as identified by proclamations — but rather whenever organizations warrant attention for worthy activities.

■ Coordinate coverage of activities scheduled in conjunction with proclamations. For example, be aware that several nursing homes might forward news releases in conjunction with Long-Term Care Week and each will be seeking publicity.

■ Focus on coverage of events, not just promotion. Newspapers have limited resources to cover all events, and these events often are static and do not lend themselves to a photo: i.e. a booth at a shopping mall publicizing American Heart Association Month.

■ Some proclamations do in fact deserve attention, especially if they are observed communitywide. National Volunteer Recognition Week, complete with honoring a city's top volunteer, is an example.

Consistency

It's become commonplace for organizations to issue proclamations as a public relations tool. Newspapers must be aware that if they publish one proclamation, other groups will seek similar treatment.

Communication

Contributions of community groups are important to local quality of life. Their work should be recognized and publicized. How newspapers do this should be clearly communicated to groups in order to avoid hard feelings and misunderstanding.

Public employees/elected officials

Premise

Public employees and elected officials are held to a higher level of accountability by virtue of the fact that taxes pay their salaries. Publishing information such as salaries and job performance fall under a newspaper's watchdog role.

Parameters

■ Employee salary negotiations and settlements should be monitored and reported at appropriate times. Salary/benefit packages usually represent the lion's share of a local government's budget.

■ Terms of union contracts usually are spelled out for the group as a whole. Terms of supervisor contracts should be spelled out for each individual.

■ Salaries should be published when individuals are hired, particularly for supervisory and management personnel.

■ Salaries should be published if they are "in the news" — e.g., a new contract or an employee wage study. They should not be published simply in response to a reader's query.

■ Discipline of public employees should be reported.

■ In a similar vein, citations for superlative performance should be recognized.

■ Public employees have private lives, too, and newspapers must be sensitive to when criticism is off limits for publication. For example, it's legitimate for a reader to comment on an unkempt rental property of an elected official. But it's not appropriate to publish criticism on an off-color comment made by the official at a private party.

■ Discretion should be used when a public employee or elected official breaks the law. The citation might warrant an article, depending on the law broken and the individual's level of responsibility.

Consistency

Newsrooms must strive for the same level of scrutiny of all public employees and elected officials. That requires close monitoring of all government bodies such as schools, counties and cities.

Communication

Most of this information is public under state laws. Make sure government bodies are aware of the laws. Newspapers will have better luck getting information if they routinely recognize the "good" and "bad" news that comes out of City Hall.

Public records

Premise

Public records are the pulse of community life — whether the records are building permits, marriage licenses, bankruptcies, traffic tickets or court sentences.

Parameters

■ Decide which public records to publish, then develop processes to do so on a regular and consistent basis.

■ One person — usually the editor — should field all requests from individuals who ask to have public records withheld from publication. Be cognizant that no matter how compelling a request — even if it comes from a friend or associate — consistency must be the norm.

■ Withholding publication of public records must be the rare exception if newspapers are to have credible policies. Double standards are unacceptable.

■ Reporting of public records must be timely and complete. That requires working on two fronts: meeting with appropriate public officials and devoting appropriate staff resources.

■ A democratic system depends on public knowledge of all public records — those considered both "good" and "bad" by the affected individuals.

■ Publication of certain public records demands attention from start to finish of a process. For example, in court cases, it's not sufficient to simply report individuals have been charged with a crime. Follow-up is mandatory — reporting whether individuals were found innocent or found guilty, and the accompanying sentence.

Consistency
It's unfair to put editors in the position of being judge and jury on whether reasons are compelling enough to withhold records. A policy riddled with double standards is no policy at all.

Communication
The policy should be communicated to those who routinely oversee public records — i.e,. law enforcement personnel and officials at city hall and the courthouse. Editors must be consistent in explaining decisions and rationale to readers.

Sports suspensions

Premise
Newspapers devote a great deal of resources to reporting high school sports and in many cases are boosters of teams and individual athletes. Readers also deserve to know when individuals are unable to participate — whether due to injury, sickness, family emergency, discipline or violation of participation rules.

Parameters
■ Report suspensions for any player on any varsity team — whether a starter or a reserve.

■ Keep reports brief — usually two or three sentences — and include information within the report of the first contest the player misses. Identify the player, the reason for the suspension — e.g., violation of local school district or high school league rules, and the length of the suspension.

■ Newspapers may decide to further identify the nature of the suspension: e.g., academic reasons or violation of drug/alcohol rules.

■ Make it clear when players are being disciplined for second or third offenses, and note the accompanying penalties.

■ In general, do not go to extra lengths to report when suspended players return to a lineup.

■ Suspensions of players on non-varsity teams usually will not be reported.

■ Many suspensions are common knowledge. Nonetheless, newspapers must get confirmation of all suspensions — whether it's on the record or off the record — prior to publication. Keep reports timely, reporting suspensions as they occur and not days or weeks after the fact.

Consistency
The policy should apply to all sports teams within readership areas. It's unrealistic, however, to expect that staffs will be aware of all suspensions.

Communication
The policy should be distributed to all schools. Newspapers also might consider alerting sports booster clubs to the policy.

Suicides

Premise
Deaths should be identified that are the result of other than natural causes. Reporting of suicides also requires greater sensitivity than deaths of other unnatural causes — for example, drowning or murder. Cause of death is a public record in most states.

Parameters
■ Identify suicide as the cause of death in a story separate from the formal obituary.

■ Report the suicide on a page separate from the obituaries. Most reports should be on an inside page.

■ Identify the cause of death — e.g., self-inflicted gun wound — to squelch rumors.

■ Avoid using the word "suicide" in the headline or text.

■ Report suicides promptly — as quickly as information is confirmed by authorities. Report all suicides that occur in readership area. Do not restrict reports of suicides to those that occur in "public" areas or suicides by individuals deemed "public" figures.

■ Keep reports brief, unless there are extenuating circumstances. In general, other information about the individuals — personal background, survivors — should be placed in the formal obituary.

Consistency

Getting information in a timely fashion can be the biggest hindrance to reporting suicides. Authorities often are unwilling or uncomfortable in reporting the cause of death, even when it's deemed a public record. That means some suicides might necessarily be reported after the fact — after funerals — further aggravating a family's grief. Newspapers must be aggressive in confirming suicides.

Communication

The policy should be made clear with law enforcement agencies, so everyone has a common understanding of the information being sought under state law. Funeral homes also should be alerted so they can alert families to the policy.

Weddings/civil unions

Premise

Weddings are special moments in people's lives. Policies must recognize the changing social norms of marriage — specifically, civil unions.

Parameters

■ Legally recognized unions between a man and woman will be reported as "marriages."

■ Unions between two individuals of the same sex will be reported as "civil unions."

■ Timely reports — those submitted within 10 weeks of the ceremony — will include more detailed information and a photo.

■ Reports submitted beyond 10 weeks after the ceremony will include only basic information and will not include a photo.

■ For timely reports, the following details will be reported: bride and bridegroom — educational background, employer, names of parents, individual performing ceremony, the bridal party — names of all members of bridal party, including their city of residence and relationship to bride and groom.

■ For reports that are submitted beyond the 10-week deadline, the following basic information will be reported: name of bride and groom and their current residence; their parents; date and location of ceremony.

■ Color or black-and-white photos will be accepted, but all photos will be reproduced in black-and-white.

■ No announcements will be accepted without the name and contact of the person submitting the announcement.

Consistency
Marriages are among those hometown news items where individuals scrutinize how other reports are handled. Exceptions should be allowed only in extenuating circumstances.

Communication
Wedding policies should be published regularly. Copies also should be distributed to sites where individuals apply for marriage licenses, and at other appropriate businesses — e.g., bridal stores.

Index

117

If you found this book useful, please visit the website of Marion Street Press, Inc. for more outstanding books for journalists:

www.marionstreetpress.com

Other journalism titles from Marion Street Press, Inc.

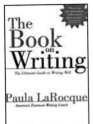

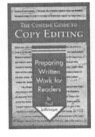